COMMON MAN'S GUIDE
To
Police and Criminal Laws

Attention Authors

COMMON MAN'S GUIDE
TO
Police and Criminal Laws

Dr DV Guruprasad, IPS
Director General of Police
Karnataka

Manas Publications
(We Convert Fighters into Writers)
New Delhi-110002 (INDIA)

MANAS PUBLICATIONS
(We Convert Fighters into Writers)
(Publishers-Library Suppliers-Importers & Exporters)
4402/5-A, Ansari Road (Opp. HDFC Bank)
Darya Ganj, New Delhi - 110 002 (India)
Phones: Off.: 011-23260783, 23265523, Res.: 011-23842660
E-mail: manaspublications@gmail.com
manaspublications@yahoo.com
Website: www.manaspublications.in

New Impression 2016 (FP-2011)

ISBN : 978-81-7049- 385-3

Rs. 295/-

Designed at
Manas Publications

Printed in India at
RK Print Services, Delhi
and published by Mrs Suman Lata for
Manas Publications, 4402/5-A,
Ansari Road, (Opp HDFC Bank),
Darya Ganj, New Delhi - 110002 (INDIA)

Preface

It has been my firm belief that police has to actively work in cooperation with the public it serves. Many misconceptions about police in public mind are only due to lack of awareness on the part of public about police and their functioning. Even after 60 years of independence, common man (even an educated man), is afraid to enter a police station. He feels that he would be put to lot of trouble by the police even if he is innocent. Therefore, public keep police at an arms length and interact with the police only if it is unavoidable. Because of the lack of interaction between police and public there are lots of doubts in the minds of public about various laws and procedures dealt with by the police. I will not be wrong if I say that this public ignorance is easily exploited by some unscrupulous police officers and men to further their own selfish ends.

My endeavour has always been to empower the common man with the knowledge of police procedures and criminal laws. I sincerely feel that once the citizen is aware of various legal provisions he will not be scared to visit a police station and he will not be easily exploited by unscrupulous and corruptive elements in the police force. Therefore I have been giving regular lectures and have been regularly writing articles both in English and in my mother tongue Kannada on subjects related to police and criminal law to educate the common man.

"New Indian Express" and "Vijaya Karnataka", two leading newspapers of Bangalore, approached me to answer queries they receive from the public on matters relating to police. For a period of more than 3 years I answered questions received from common man about various aspects of criminal law and police. The book which is in your hand is collection of these columns published in the above dailies.

Since Indian Penal Code and Criminal Procedure Code are common for the entire country even though the answers may be in respect of questions raised by the readers of Karnataka, they can easily be applicable to the question of a reader from any part of India. I hope that this endeavour would be useful to the readers.

I am grateful to both Smt. Ramya Latha and Smt. Hemalatha, my secretaries who have toiled hard to type out this work. My wife Swarna, Son Sumkh and Daughter Apoorva have always given constructive criticism about my work. I am grateful to all of them.

Dr. DV Guruprasad
Director General of Police,
Karnataka

CITIZEN'S QUESTIONS ANSWERED BY DGP

Q: What is meant by an FIR?

– Sushma

A: FIR means the First Information Report, which is the foundation of any criminal case. Whenever a Police Station receives a report of commission of any cognizable offence, it is the duty of the Station House Officer of the Police Station to record the information, proceed to the place of offence and commence the investigation. In other words, FIR is the first and most important document in the investigation of a criminal case.

Q: Are there any classification among cases to be investigated by the Police?

– R.K. Sharma

A: There are mainly two types of cases; Civil and Criminal. Civil cases are such cases concerning civil wrongs. For example, dispute regarding properties. These cases have to be settled in civil courts. Criminal cases are those cases in which police are empowered to investigate. For example, cases of theft, dacoity, murder, causing hurt etc. Even among criminal cases there are two types - Cognizable and Non-cognizable. Cognizable cases are those in which police draw up an FIR, register a case and arrest the accused without

getting a warrant from a Magistrate. In non-cognizable cases police can take up investigation only as per the direction of the courts. A simple example of non-cognizable case, is verbal abuse, or hitting a person by hand and causing him simple injury. There is also a third category of cases, which are traffic offences. In some of these cases FIR is drawn and in some other cases, criminal cases are not registered. For example for driving without license, jumping of traffic signals etc no case is registered. However, in cases where injuries/death are caused in motor vehicle accidents cases are registered.

Q: If the police don't register a case, is there any remedy?

– S.K. Srivastava

A: As per the Criminal Procedure Code, whenever information relating to commission of a cognizable offence is given to an Officer of a police station, he is bound to register a case and give a copy of the FIR free of cost to the complainant. However, if any police officer refuses to register such a complaint, the aggrieved party may send the complaint in writing by post to the SP or the DCP concerned. If the superior officer is satisfied that the complaint discloses commission of a cognizable offence, he shall get the case registered and investigated by any officer subordinate to him. If the superior officer also does not take any action, the complainant can approach a magistrate having jurisdiction over the area and lodge a complaint before him. The magistrate can refer such complaint for investigation by the police, in which case an FIR is drawn.

Q: Some time back I had gone to a Police Station stating that my dog has been stolen by my neighbour. Police refused to register this complaint. Are they right in doing this?

– Priyanka Sood

A: If a police officer, after receipt of a complaint of a cognizable case, feels that the case in hand is not of a serious nature or if he believes that there is no sufficient ground for investigation of that case he may refuse to take up investigation of the case. However, he is bound to inform the complainant the reasons for refusal to take up the case.

Q: How can a person get police to investigate a non-cognizable case?

— Rakesh Mishra

A: If a person goes to a police station to report a non-cognizable offence, the police officer will inform the person that since the case is non-cognizable, he cannot register an FIR and investigate. When this happens, the complainant can approach the Court directly and lodge his complaint. The court in turn can direct the police to investigate the case. Sometimes, the police can also themselves request the court to permit them to take up investigation of a non-cognizable offence case and if the court consents investigate it.

Sometimes, there may be several acts in a transaction. One of the acts can turn into a non-cognizable offence and another may turn into a cognizable offence. For example, if a person abuses another using vulgar language, it amounts to a non-cognizable offence. However, if the same person after using vulgar language forcibly enters into the victim's house and continues to abuse him, the action of forcible entry into the house with a criminal intention will be a cognizable offence. Hence, in this transaction since two acts are contained, one of which amounts to cognizable offence, police can take up the case and investigate.

Q: Can police put behind bars anyone whom they want to?

— Suraj Kashyap

A: By the phrase "putting behind bars", if you mean arrest, it is not possible for the police to arrest any person without a proper reason. While a police officer can call any person (except woman and children) to the police station for the purposes of investigation, it is not easy to arrest any person on the whims and fancy of a Police Officer. The Criminal Procedure Code has recently been amended and new provisions in respect of arrest have been inserted. Any contravention of these provisions or any contravention of Human Rights by the police can be complained against.

Q: What is meant by bail?

– Sudarshan

A: Whenever a person is arrested by the police, he cannot be permanently kept under custody. An arrested person, if involved in a bailable offence, shall be released by the police after observing certain formalities. Bailable offences are normally non-serious offences. Non-bailable offences on the other hand are offences like murder, dacoity, dowry death, rape etc. For example, while driving a car if a person hits a scooterist and the scooterist has fractured his legs, the accused will be arrested by the police but released on bail. However, if a person is accused of rape, which is a non-bailable offence, the accused will not be released by police. For his bail he has to approach the concerned Court.

Q: Why is that even after a thief is caught, the entire stolen property is not recovered by the police?

– Y.N. Mahajan

A: Thieves normally steal three kinds of property: Cash, gold, silver ornaments and goods like Camera, T.V, Mobile phone etc. If a thief steals cash, he blows up the stolen cash in a very short period of time. If he steals ornaments he will go to a receiver of stolen

property and sell them and the receiver in turn melts the gold or silver. Because of this, it is virtually not possible to recover stolen cash and ornaments intact. By the time the police catch the culprit, he would not be having the stolen property with him. Hence, even after a theft case is detected the entire property stolen cannot be recovered. However, if the stolen goods are TV/VCR/Car etc the property can be recovered intact. Sometimes, stolen cars are also cannibalised and the spare parts are sold.

Q: After police recover the stolen property what should a victim do to get his property back?

– Sneha Tripathy

A: Normally after police recover the stolen property from the culprit, the complainant/victim is called to the police station to identify the property. Once the property is identified, the complainant can request the magistrate to allow him to take back the property, promising the magistrate that the property will be produced as and when required by the Court. Normally Courts grant permission to the police to return the recovered stolen property to the complainant.

Q: Some of my friends say that though police recover a large chunk of stolen property, they misappropriate a portion of the recovered property for their own use. Is it true?

– Vibha Bhatnagar

A: This type of allegation has been heard time and again. One cannot rule out the possibility of some unscrupulous investigating officers misappropriating a part of the recovered stolen property for their own use. Whenever, such instances have come to light, strictest disciplinary action has been taken against errant police officers. We can also book them under criminal laws.

Q: Is it not necessary for the police to keep women police whenever they call a woman to the police station either for enquiry or as an accused?

– Neha Kamath

A: As per the Criminal Procedure Code, if a child or woman is required as a witness in any criminal case, such person cannot be called to the police station. On the other hand, the investigating officer should go to the residence of the witness and record the statement. If a woman is to be arrested by the police, as far as possible a woman police officer should be present. If there is no woman officer, a male police officer cannot even touch the woman to be arrested. A woman is normally not detained in a police lock up between dusk and dawn. In case such a detention is inevitable, a woman police officer shall invariably be present near the person arrested. A number of laws are in place to ensure the dignity of the arrested woman.

Q: A few days back some police officers came to my house and stated that they have to search my house in connection with a case they are investigating. What are the provisions of search?

– Sumithra Sawant

A: Normally search can be conducted by officers belonging to Police, Income tax, Customs, Forest Departments etc. However, before allowing any person entry into your premises you must make sure that they are government officials and authorized to conduct search. You have to verify their identity cards. Normally officers conducting search will have warrant of search issued by a competent Court of Law. You will have to ask the searching party to show you the search warrant and verify whether the warrant contains your name and correct address of your premises. You will have to sign on the copy of the warrant shown to you. Sometimes officers can conduct search even without a warrant. Before allowing entry

into your house you have to ask each and all the officers to subject themselves for search. This precaution is to prevent the searching party to bring and place incriminating articles in your house. After ensuring that the searching party does not have any incriminating articles they can be allowed ingress into the house. The searching party will have to observe all decency and decorum while conducting search. After the search, the search party has to prepare a panchanama. If the party is seizing any articles from your house, the search list of the articles seized is to be prepared by them. For example if they seize a gold ring weighing 20 gms, the same has to be mentioned in the list. A copy of the mahajar panchanama along with a copy of the search list has to be given to you. You will have to sign the duplicate copy of the panchanama which will be with the search party. During the house search you are not bound to provide any food/refreshments to the searching party. The searching party will have to consist of two independent panch witnesses. They can be allowed to take the seized articles as per the search list given to you.

Sometimes searches are conducted only for the purposes of finding out weapons of offence, evidence related to the crime like documents etc. Apart from house search investigating agencies are also authorized to conduct personal searches. While conducting personal search decency and decorum need to be observed. A woman has to be searched only by a woman officer. A woman can refuse to be searched by a male person.

If a police officer who has the authority to arrest a person believes that the person he is looking for is hiding in a place he can search the premises in question and if you are the occupant of such a premises you are bound to allow access to the police to conduct the search. Police officers are also authorized to forcibly break into any house and conduct search to prevent

escape by the person who is evading arrest. However, if there are any *purdahnashin* ladies present in the house, the police officer should give notice to such females that they are at liberty to withdraw before going into the house and then enter the house.

Q: What is the difference between a summon and warrant?

– Shamsher Singh

A: A summon is a direction by a Court of Law to a person to attend the Court. Every summon issued by a Court will be in writing, will be in duplicate and will be signed by the presiding officer of the Court and shall be having the seal of the Court. Normally a police officer will serve the summon on a person. If you are summoned by a Court you are expected to get a copy of the summon from the policeman and sign the duplicate copy for having received the summon. Summon need to be served personally. It is sometimes sent through post, sent to a government servant through his or her superiors etc. A summon can be pasted on the door of the house of the person summoned. It can also be served through an adult male member of the household.

A warrant, on the other hand is a direction of the Court to a public servant to arrest someone. If a person who receives a summon disregards the same and does not attend the Court, a warrant is normally issued to compel his appearance in the Court. If it is a bailable warrant, the police officer will arrest you, and then release you on bail and ask you to appear in the court on the date mentioned in the warrant. If it is a non-bailable warrant, a police officer will show the warrant to you, arrest you and produce you before the Court. When you are produced in the Court, it is for the Court either to release you on bail or keep you in judicial custody. If you are an accused for criminal case, depending on the gravity of the case you may be bailed out or sent to prison.

Q: When can a police arrest a person? What are the rights of the arrested person?

– Hemamalini

A: A police officer is empowered to arrest, without any warrant from a competent court, any person who is suspected to have committed an offence in the presence of a police officer [offences like theft, dacoity, murder, rape, receiving stolen property, voluntarily causing hurt etc]

As per the amended Criminal Procedure Code, a police officer can arrest any person against whom a reasonable complaint has been made for an offence for which there is an imprisonment for a term extending more than 7 years. The police officer can arrest him only if he is satisfied that the arrest is necessary to prevent such a person from committing any further offence or to prevent that person to tamper with evidence.

Every police officer while making arrest is expected to disclose his identity to the arrested person. When he is arresting a person he has to issue a memo of arrest which is to be attested by either a family member of the arrested person or a respectable member of the locality. The arrested person is expected to counter sign this memo of arrest. While effecting arrest the police officer has to inform the person arrested the reasons for the arrest. The arrested person should also be allowed to meet an advocate of his choice during his custody by the police.

A male police officer shall not touch a female while making her arrest. Immediately after a person is arrested, the arrested person shall be subjected to a medical examination. A copy of the medical report shall be given to the arrested person. The person arrested shall be produced within 24 hours of his arrest before the Magistrate.

Q: I run a small business establishment. The other day some persons carrying a TV camera barged into my room and started asking me questions stating that they are from a news channel. I refused to answer. Can media persons barge into private premises? Who has given them license?

— Arun Kumar

A: No person is authorized to forcibly enter into any premises without the permission of the occupant of the premises. If a person forcibly enters private premises it will amount to criminal trespass. As per Section 441 of the IPC, whoever enters into property in possession of another, with an intent to commit an offence, or intimidate, or annoy the person in possession of such property, is said to commit criminal trespass. Since the media persons entered your premises with an intention to annoy or intimidate you, you can file a case against the concerned for an offence of trespass under section 447 IPC, which is a cognizable offence.

Q: I purchased a flat in a huge apartment block which consists of 100 flats. I am one of the 39 persons who have taken possession of my flat. The remaining 61 persons are getting their flats altered. The alteration being undertaken by the other flat owners is causing lot of annoyance to us, who are already living in the flats. We are having terrible noise pollution. Can something be done about this?

— N. Sujendra

A: Criminal action cannot be taken against the other flat owners who are causing noise pollution. You may probably have a meeting with them and request them not to disturb you at specific time. You may approach Pollution Control Board authorities in this regard and complaint.

Q: The other day I travelled to Delhi by car and in the city a drunken driver came and hit my parked car

and sped away. I could not note down the car number since the letters and numerals were in Devanagiri and I am from a Southern State. Is it lawful to use number plates in regional languages?

– Navneet Krishnan

A: It is not legal to have vehicle number plates written in languages other than English and numerals other than Roman. It is the duty of the police as well as the transport department to book people who flout this rule. There is a move to have common type of vehicle number plates for the entire country.

Q: It is seen that some reporters of TV channels are at the places of some scenes of crime, especially regarding riot and assault and cover the event live. Does this not amount to being co-accused? Why can't police take action against such journalists?

– S. Shrikanth

A: It needs to be proved during investigation that the journalist in question actively aided and abetted the commission of a crime. Without this proof, it is not possible to make a journalist co-accused in the crime merely because he was at the scene of crime when crime was happening.

Q: I pay my electricity bills through my bank and on due date payment is made. However the electricity supply company has disconnected electricity to my flat without intimating me ostensibly for the reason that I did not pay my dues. Can I take up a criminal case against the Electric Company?

– B. B. L. Gupta

A: This is not a matter coming under the purview of criminal law. Please approach the Consumer Forum.

Q: About 20 slum dwellers have put up their huts in a vacant plot in front of my house since 8 months. My

complaints to the municipal authorities have gone unheeded. Can police help?

– L. Dwivedi

A: If the owner of the vacant plot gives a complaint of trespass against the slum dwellers, a case can be taken up. Please find out the owner of the plot and ask him to lodge a FIR.

Q: A woman aged 32 years had enticed my son aged 20 years and both of them have got married in a temple. Can I lodge a criminal complaint against the woman?

– Bharathi

A: Since your son is above 18 years of age, the act of the woman in question does not amount to either abduction or kidnapping as defined in the IPC. However if a man is unlawfully married to a woman who dishonestly goes through the ceremony of being married, he can be punished with imprisonment up to 7 years. In the case of your son this section of law [Sec.496 IPC] does not apply because he would become an accused if you give a complaint. Also as per Child Marriage Restraint Act 1921, if a male below 21 years marries a female below 18 years the male would be punishable. This also does not apply.

Q: I have a peculiar problem with my neighbour. When branches of two trees in my compound went across to his compound, he filed a case in the Court and got an order to cut down the trees. Subsequently, he picked up a quarrel stating that because of the roots of my trees, his compound wall has collapsed and he has suffered damage. Now he is throwing chemicals on my plants and destroying them. Can I take up a criminal case against him?

– Reeta L

A: The action of your neighbour is an offence of mischief. It is however, non-cognizable and hence police cannot register an FIR. You have to approach a Court.

Q: In my locality a large number of wine shops have been opened. Many customers of the shops are consuming liquor on the pavement openly. Many persons park their cars in front of the shops and get their supplies to the cars. It is as if the wine store is a drive-in hotel. To whom should I complain?

– S. Babu

A: You may complain to the Excise Commissioner. If the clients of the wine shop are causing nuisance, you may report the matter to the jurisdictional police station.

Q: A few years ago, my scooter dashed against a cyclist and a case was filed against me. I paid a fine of Rs.500/- in the Court. I am told that because of my involvement in this case, getting government job is difficult. Is this true?

– Name withheld

A: Before appointing any person for a government job his character and antecedents are verified by the police. During such verification your involvement in this case will come out. Hence it is advisable for you to mention in your job application form that you were fined for an offence. I personally feel that conviction in a case of rash and negligent driving should not come in the way of government appointment, as it is not a case of moral turpitude.

Q: I got married 3 years ago. My wife, it seems, was in love with a classmate of hers and was not willing to marry me. However, due to the pressure from her family she got married to me. Every day she is in touch with her boy friend and moves out with him at odd hours. Whenever I protest she says that she will teach me a lesson by filing a case against me. I strongly suspect that she is sleeping with her boy friend. What should I do?

– Name withheld

A: While you cannot take up a case against your wife, you can take up a case against her boy friend for an offence of adultery u/s 497 IPC. Any person who has sexual intercourse with the wife of another man without the consent of that man, is guilty of adultery and shall be punishable with imprisonment up to 5 years. Since the wife cannot be punished under this section, you may contemplate divorcing her. It is also likely that she will file a case of dowry harassment against you and your parents. Necessary evidence to disprove this may be built up now itself. You may consult a lawyer.

Q: I was in love with a classmate of mine. We wanted to get married but she married someone else. Even after marriage she was writing love letters to me with her blood. I told her to forget me and allow me to lead my life. A few weeks ago I was called to police station wherein I was told that my former girl friend has given complaint against me for sending her obscene e-mails. The fact is that my girl friend knew the login and password details of my e-mail account and using this she has sent an obscene mail to herself. Now I am in deep trouble. What should I do?

– Name withheld

A: If the e-mail has been sent from your laptop or desktop, it is very difficult to disprove the allegations. You will have to convince the Investigating Officer about your innocence. I feel that you have been trapped and may have to face prosecution. It is always necessary to protect one's login and password particulars.

Q: I had given a loan of Rs.50,000/- to a friend and he had given an acknowledgement on a white paper affixing a revenue stamp. He had agreed to repay the loan in twelve months without interest. So far he has

not paid a penny. Whenever I ask him to return the money, he threatens me saying that he will kill me if I ask for repayment. What should I do?

– Kamalakar

A: His threat definitely amounts to a criminal case. You may lodge a complaint in the concerned police station. You should have obtained from him signed post dated cheques when you gave him the loan. You could have deposited the cheque in your bank and when it bounced, you could have taken up a case against him. You can now file a civil suit to recover the amounts due from him.

Q: Two years ago a person stating to be working in Police Department got introduced to me. We both liked each other and he promised to marry me. He took me to various places and we literally lived as husband and wife. I have now learnt that he has married someone else. Can I file a criminal case against him?

– Name withheld

A: If any man indulges in sex with a woman, promising her marriage it does not amount to an offence of rape. However, if you had given consent for sexual intercourse believing to be lawfully married to him, it would have amounted to a case of rape. In other words, if both of you had gone to a temple, exchanged garlands and believed that you both are married and after getting such a belief, if you had consented for sexual intercourse then an offence of rape could have been made out. Now nothing can be done. There is a case law in Delhi High Court that such a case will amount to cheating, but such a view is not supported by many.

Q: A person who is known to me and who is married is inserting advertisements in newspapers that he is unmarried and is in the look out for brides. Should not the police be taking action against him?

– Rekha

A: How should the police know that the person who has given the advertisement is married or otherwise? An affected party has to approach the police and inform about the cheating being indulged in. Since you know that the advertisement in question is false, you may yourself approach the police and give a complaint. Action will definitely be taken against him.

Q: Can police officers take action based on an anonymous petition?

– Nagaraj

A: Police receive hundreds of anonymous petitions daily. The normal procedure is that if an anonymous or pseudonymous petition is received and if that petition contains any specific and actionable information, the petition is enquired into. If a petition contains false allegations it will not be considered.

Q: A few months ago, there was a protest against government in our town regarding water shortage. Some people encircled the Tehsil office and were throwing stones. I was passing by and was watching what was happening. Police lathi charged the crowd in which I was injured. I got treated in a hospital for the injury. Now I have received summons from the Court as an accused, even though I am innocent and was injured. Why a false case is filed against me?

– Pritam Singh

A: Normally in a law and order situation it is the bystanders who are affected. Because of your curiosity you have got into trouble. The fact that you were injured in a police lathi charge establishes that you were part of a mob that pelted stones on a government office. You will have to face prosecution.

Q: Can we register our complaints on line?

– Keshi. S.G.

A: For the time being it is not possible to register complaints on line. It requires amendment to certain laws. Soon it may happen.

Q: I got a text message on my cell phone stating that I have won one million pounds and was asked to contact an e-mail ID. When I sent a mail I was asked to send my personal details. Is this some type of fraud?

– Nischay. M.

A: No one can win a lottery unless he participates in the same by buying a ticket. If a person wins a lottery, he is expected to pay necessary income tax. The very fact that an unknown person has sent a SMS stating you have won a lottery and the fact that he is asking you to provide personal details is indicative that this is a scam. A large number of persons have lost millions of rupees by responding to such messages. The moment you get such messages delete the same. It is very difficult to bring to book such scamsters.

Q: I had a problem with my neighbour. I was called to the police station. My neighbour had also come to the station. The officer asked me to write on a paper stating that I will not cause any problem to my neighbour. Accordingly, I wrote a statement, signed it and gave it to the Inspector. Will I get into some trouble for doing so? Will this statement be used against me to prevent me from getting a government job?

– Shravan Gambhir

A: You might have been called to the police station to enquire into a complaint by your neighbour. This may be concerning a petty/non-cognizable case. I don't think you will get into any trouble by giving an undertaking in the police station.

Q: About 30 years ago, I befriended a person who was of my father's age. He was unmarried and I used to assist him. Over the years, he developed fondness

towards me and recently he wrote his will stating that all his immovable property should go to me. Most of his relatives are dead. My friend is having bout of depression of late. Last week he purchased some sleeping tablets and tried to consume them. By chance I noticed them and threw them away. Supposing my friend commits suicide, will I get into any trouble with the Police?

— Garima Goel

A: It is most likely that the finger of suspicion will point towards you, if your friend faces an unnatural death. I presume that the will executed by your friend has been registered and is not a fresh one. If there are witnesses to state that you have been looking after the old gentleman for decades and that you had no ulterior motives, you may not get into any problem.

Q: I was in love with a boy. For some reason our relationship soured. Now I am engaged to be married. My fiancé is getting a number of anonymous letters, wherein all sorts of false imputations about my character is being made. My fiancé is also getting anonymous calls asking him to break the marriage. I strongly suspect my former boy friend to be doing this. Can I complain to police?

— Suguna

A: As per the existing laws, no criminal offence is made out and hence police cannot take any action in this regard.

Q: I am having a live-in relationship with a colleague of mine since the two years. I have learnt recently that she is having a physical relationship with another colleague. Can I complain against her?

— Name withheld

A: Since you have not married the woman in question, if another person has sexual intercourse with the woman it does not amount to adultery as defined in IPC. Hence police cannot take action.

Q: I am living in an apartment block located near a lake. Local people fish in this lake. Recently lot of fish in the lake died and villagers are holding us responsible. They state that the sewage water of our apartments has entered the lake and killed the fish. The villages have threatened that they will sit on strike in front of our gate and will not allow us to go out. What action can be taken?

—B. Kiran

A: Please first establish the cause of death of the fish in the lake. If the sewage water of your colony is the cause, rectify the same. Every person has a right to protest peacefully. However, if the villagers block the entry and exit of your apartment, a criminal case of wrongful restraint and wrongful confinement can be made out. I suggest you sort out this problem by mutual discussion.

Q: My house was burgled nine months ago. I lodged a complaint; police registered the case, came to my house, conducted spot inspection, took some finger prints and then went away. Till today, I don't know the stage of the investigation. Is their any time limit to finalize investigation of a case?

— Ram Prasad

A: After a criminal case is registered by the police, investigation will proceed, as contemplated under the Criminal Procedure Code. In a case of theft it is not possible to detect the same in a time frame. Therefore, if after 5-6 months the case is not detected, the police file a report with the magistrate stating that the case is not detected, as and when the case is detected, the closed case is reopened.

If the accused is arrested and detained in the custody, the investigation of the case needs to be completed within a maximum period of 60 or 90 days depending upon the offence. If the investigation is not

finalized by this time frame, the detained accused will be released on bail.

Normally after finalization of investigation the investigating officer is bound to inform the complainant, the result of the investigation. If the case is undetected a notice about the same is given to the complainant. Similarly, if the case is closed as mistake of fact also a notice is given. After receipt of this notice, the complainant can contest the notice in Court of law and comment on the investigation of the case.

Now-a-days, various police forces in the country are giving SMS alerts regarding progress of the investigation to the complainants.

Q: If a person is arrested in a dowry death case. Can he be released on bail?

– Rehana

A: Any person accused in a dowry death case, which is non-bailable offence will naturally be sent to judicial custody. If the police file charge sheet in the case within 90 days the accused will continue to be in custody. Otherwise the accused will be released on bail. While in custody the accused is also entitled to approach Courts and request for bail. Sometimes, such requests are considered and the accused is set free. Many High Courts have held that in dowry harassment cases, police should effect arrests only if strong evidence is available against the accused.

Q: Our servant, who stole gold ornaments from our house, confessed to his crime before the police. He was imprisoned. I am now told that he has been acquitted of the case. Even though he confessed to his crime why was he acquitted?

– Vikram Taneja

A: A confession before a police officer is not treated as evidence in a Court of Law. If your servant had

confessed to his crime during the course of the trial, probably he might have been convicted. However, as per our constitution no person accused of any offence can be compelled to be a witness against himself. Also, every person is said to be innocent till proved guilty in a Court of Law. Probably, the prosecution could not prove the guilt of your servant in the Court.

Q: A relative of mine is accused in a false case of dowry harassment filed by his wife. His passport was impounded by the police. Now he has to go abroad on a business trip. Can he get his passport back?

– Omkar Thakur

A: Your relative, through his advocate can give an application to the Court requesting him to allow to go abroad on business. If he convinces the Court of his intention to return to India and face the trial, the court is likely to agree to his request.

Q: I was running a business with a friend, he cheated me to the tune of '. 20 lakhs. I filed a case against him. He was arrested and later let off on bail. Now he has run away and I am told he is living in some other city. How can I make him to face the Court?

– Rajat Gupta

A: You can inform the prosecution the whereabouts of the accused. The Court will then issue a warrant in his name and direct the police officers of the city where he is now living to execute the warrant to arrest him and bring before the Court. Suppose a person absconds from the clutches of law, he can be declared as a proclaimed offender and his property can be attached by the Court.

Q: One of my relative was arrested by the police. His wife requested me to stand surety for his bail. Accordingly, I gave surety. Now my friend has

absconded and the police are troubling me to trace him. What can I do?

— Ram Vilas

A: Since you have given a surety for bailing out your relative, it becomes your duty to get the person before law. Whatever the amount that has been mentioned in the surety will have to be paid by you. You may also be liable to be fined.

Q: Can police handcuff a person?

— Piyush Goenka

A: The Supreme Court has repeatedly ruled that no arrested person should be handcuffed and paraded in public and that such acts violate human dignity. The National Human Rights Commission has also directed that the arrested person should not be hand cuffed. However, handcuffing can be resorted if the person concerned is a dangerous criminal.

Q: My friend who is a doctor runs a nursing home. A few days ago one of his patients died, immediately thereafter the victim's relative lodged a police complaint. Police arrested the doctor and filed a case against him. How can the police determine whether the doctor is actually responsible for the death?

— Meer Ahamed Hussain

A: It is definitely difficult for the police to establish whether a death that has occurred in a hospital / nursing home is due to the negligence of the doctor concerned or otherwise. The Supreme Court has ruled that police cannot arrest doctors over complaints of medical negligence without prima-facie evidence. The court has also stated that complaint of medical negligence on the part of any doctor needs to be referred to a panel of experts in the field before taking action. Hence the action of the police in arresting your doctor friend is not justified.

Q: When I was returning to my hostel last night, one car came from behind and hit me. I fell down but did not sustain any serious injuries. The driver and the other occupants in the car were dead drunk. I alerted the police control room through my cell phone and very soon a police van came to the spot. Seeing that no one was injured and seeing that the vehicles were also not damaged, the police officer allowed the car to go away. I am certain that he has taken a bribe from the culprit. What should I do?

– Monarch Sharma

A: Whenever an accident takes place it is necessary that a complaint is immediately lodged with the police. You have only mentioned about the accident to the control room. Since the police officer who came to the spot has not taken any action, you should give a written complaint about the accident to the nearest traffic police station. I hope you have noted down the registration number of the car that hit you.

Q: The other day, I was travelling in a bus and during the course of the journey I noticed that my suitcase was stolen. In the very next bus stand, I got down and went to the police station to lodge a complaint. The police there did not take up the case and advised me to give the complaint at the place where I boarded the bus. Where exactly should I lodge my complaint?

– Vineet Sahai

A: It is not necessary to give the complaint only at the place where you boarded the bus. Since the offence has taken place during the journey, any police station which falls on the route, that is any place which is the boarding point and the alighting points and places in-between can register the case and investigate.

Q: What is meant by curfew?

– Ram Goel

A: In the Criminal Procedure Code, there is no term called curfew. However, as per Sec. 144 of the CrPC, a magistrate, may, by a written order direct any person to abstain from doing a certain act. Under this provision of law a magistrate can ban assembly of persons, people carrying of arms, regulate routes of procession etc such a ban commonly known as 'Curfew'.

Q: I am an accused in a criminal case and the trial has just started. The judge in this case is from the same village from which I hail and we are not in good terms right from the beginning. I have a suspicion that this judge will definitely send me to jail. What can I do to prevent this?

– Name withheld

A: Normally, judicial officers don't hear cases wherein the accused or the victim or the lawyer for the accused is closely known to them. They recuse themselves from the case. Since you have a suspicion towards the judge in question, you can file an application before the High Court and request that your case be transferred to some other criminal court, since you don't expect a fair or impartial trial from the existing judge. If the High Court is convinced about your argument it can transfer the case to some other judge.

Q: I am running a small beauty parlour. A week back, two middle aged women came to the parlour and asked me for hair cut. I was alone at the parlour. After I cut the hair of one woman, the other woman said that she does not want any hair cut and both of them went away. Sometime later I noted that costly cosmetics, perfumes etc have been knocked away. I suspect that one of the woman has stolen them. When I went to the police station they did not believe me and refused to register an FIR. What should I do?

A: If you are very sure that these two women have committed theft of your cosmetics etc you may lodge a case of theft. If the local police are not registering a case, you may approach the higher authorities or the Court. It is very difficult to nail the culprits because all cosmetics are packed similarly and the stolen property is unidentifiable. Even if a case is registered, detecting it will be difficult.

Q: My friend was working in a massage parlour. A month ago, the owner of the parlour asked her to give massage treatment for male customers. She refused stating that she will treat only females. The owner threatened her that if she does not do as ordered, she will lose her job. She refused the request and was thrown out of her job. Can a police case be made against the parlour owner?

—Savitha

A: There are any number of massage parlours which are working as front for brothels. Is the massage parlour in question a seedy joint? Did the massage parlour owner force your friend into commercial sex? If that is the case, criminal action can be taken. If the massage parlour is actually giving treatment, this incident will not come under the purview of criminal law.

Q: My paternal uncle secretly mortgaged my parental property to a bank in 1997. We came to know about this only in 2004. When enquired with my uncle he said that we could help him clear the loan and get back the property. I agreed and contributed for the recovery of loan and interest. Despite our best efforts we are unable to clear the loan. Can I take legal action against my uncle?

—Name withheld on request

A: A bank would not have accepted the mortgage of a property if your uncle didn't really have clear title to

it. If there are joint owners for a property the consent of others for mortgage is normally taken. It is therefore not known how your uncle can secretly mortgage your ancestral property. You have not mentioned anything about your father's role in this. Why did you contribute money for loan recovery? You cannot take any criminal action against your uncle.

Q: I am an orphan and got married 3 years ago. My wife displays despicable behaviour towards one and all and uses foul languages. She is a working woman. We have a daughter and I don't want my daughter to have a disturbed childhood. My wife is also giving most of her salary to her parents and not at all contributing to run the house. When I suggested that my wife needs to be taken to a psychiatrist for her behaviour, my father-in-law said that he will file a dowry harassment case against me. My wife also threatens to commit suicide. I am totally confused. Please help.

—Lella Suji

A: Though technically your in-laws or your wife can file a dowry harassment case against you, they will have to give evidence of such harassment. Merely because a case is registered against you, you will not be straight away arrested. I would advice you to file a divorce petition. You can also collect evidence to prove that your wife is of unsound mind.

Q: Many innocent persons are being victimized in dowry harassment cases. Can't you amend the law suitably?

—V. Laxman

A: Amendment of any law has to be taken up by the Parliament. It is a fact that many innocents are being harassed in Dowry Act cases. But it is also a fact that many young women are put to untold miseries, by families which are greedy after dowry. We have to find a middle path.

Q: Outside our apartment building, two carpenter families have put a shed on the footpath. Right from morning till late at night they work in the shed and make unbearable noise. The two carpenters are also found quarrelling with each other disturbing the neighbours. What action can be taken against them?

—Sukumar

A: Action can be taken against the carpenter for a) unauthorizedly occupying public property b) Disturbance of public peace and c) Causing noise pollution. Please approach the Police, Municipal Authorities and the State Pollution Control Board.

Q: Will possession of a fake note by an individual result in immediate arrest or prosecution?

—Senthil V.

A: As per Sec 489[c] of IPC if any person is in possession of any forged currency note, fully knowing that it is forged, and intending to use the same as genuine; or if he uses the forged note as genuine, he shall be punished for a prison term which may extend to 7 years. Hence it is very clear that while mere possession a fake note is not an offence, the intention behind that possession is more important. Therefore if you happen to come to possession of a fake note, it is always advisable to destroy the same rather than trying to pass it off as genuine.

Q: Stray cattle have become a big menace on our roads. Can't the police do something about it?

—T. Syed

A: The menace of stray cattle on roads can be effectively tackled by implementing the provisions of Karnataka Police Act, Karnataka Traffic Control Act as well as Sec.289 of the Indian Penal Code. The problem that normally the police face is what to do after the animals are rounded up. Many a time ownership of these animals is difficult to establish. Many times there are

not enough places [especially in big cities] to keep the impounded animals safely. If the impounded animals are not secured, they will once again come back on the road. Unless adequate number of cattle pounds are established, this problem is difficult to tackle.

Q: I noticed an advertisement in a local newspaper wherein the advertiser is offering 5% return every month on a deposit of Rs.1 lakh. Don't you think this is fishy?

– A.Kothari

A: This definitely seems to be fishy. Before you invest your hard earned money in any financial institution, you must make sure that the concerned institution is a reputed one and it is licensed by the RBI. There are any number of fly-by-night operators who cheat the public day in and day out by offering huge returns on their investment. It is unfortunate that our public is falling pray to such unscrupulous elements repeatedly. You may confirm to the police about the company in question.

Q: I gave a complaint regarding illegal activities of a police inspector and his staff to the SP of the district. Having come to know of this, the inspector is harassing me and is threatening that he will book a false case against me and put me behind bars. What is your advice?

– K.M. Shantha Ram

A: You may lodge a complaint with the Head of Police Department as well as the Human Rights Commission. You may also lodge a complaint with the Karnataka Lokayuktha.

Q: I received a mail from www.incomemission.com stating that their mission runs a programme called Genius Technology and Consultancy Services and if I join their group I would get endless stream of income

merely by sending SMS, e-mail and postings on social media sites. Should I join?

—**T. Chandra Shekar**

A: Now-a-days many unemployed persons and housewives are generating income by sending e-mail IDS of their friends and acquaintances to some companies. I am given to understand that information so collected is sold in bulk to prospective advertisers. However, the company that you have mentioned seems to be collecting money from individuals. You should be vary of requests strangers make to you through e-mails. Check up the antecedents of the company before investing.

Q: I was driving at normal speed on a city road last week. A dog crossed my path suddenly. I applied brakes. A motor cyclist who was coming behind me at great speed hit my car from behind, fell down and injured himself. Police have filed a case against me. When I have not committed any offence, is it not unjust to book me?

—**Y.D. Bhosle**

A: Police all over the country have a habit of taking up cases against the driver of a bigger vehicle when an accident between two vehicles happens. If a bus had dashed your car from behind, a case might have been taken up against the bus driver. Mere registration of a case does not mean that you will be charged for rash and negligent driving. During the investigation if it is proved that you were driving at a normal speed and that you had to suddenly apply brakes and that the motor cyclist who dashed against you was riding at a great speed, probably you will not be sent to Court.

Q: I borrowed a lakh of rupees @ 5% per month an year ago. Since I didn't repay the principal in the prescribed

time, the rate of interest has gone up to 8% per month. I am unable to pay the interest, let alone the principal. I am now being threatened of dire consequences. Can police help?

—Name withheld

A: I guess you have borrowed money from a money lender. No person can carry on a business of money lending in Karnataka except in accordance with the licence issued to him under the Karnataka Money Lenders Act 1961. Under the same act, the Government is empowered to fix the maximum rate of interest in respect of secured and unsecured loans. Under the Karnataka Prohibition of Charging Exorbitant Interest Act 2004, no person can charge an interest of more than 18% per annum. Any person who charges interest above this rate is liable for imprisonment for a term which may extend to three years and also a fine which may extend to Rs.30,000/- Please approach the local police and complain. They will also book a case against the lender for intimidation.

Q: Is it possible to find out an absconding person? I need your help in finding an absconding person since last July 2009. Please let me know how to proceed further in this case.

—Prathi Muniyappa

A: By absconding, if you mean a missing person, you may lodge a complaint in the jurisdictional police station. In Karnataka for missing cases FIR is drawn and investigation is taken up. You have to give photograph and other details of the missing person while lodging the complaint.

Q: I have filed a dowry harassment case and domestic violence act case against my husband. Aggrieved by this, my husband made a special power of attorney, forged my signature and mortgaged the house I live

in [my husband and I are joint owners of this house] His relatives who took the house in mortgage came and occupied the house and threw me out and my young daughter. My husband has also forged my signature and converted my SB account into a joint account and has taken away all the money I had saved. Police are not helping me. What should I do?

—Bindu Reddy

A: If your husband has forged your signature on a Special Power of Attorney, you can lodge a complaint of forgery against him. He cannot mortgage the house for which you are a joint owner. You had every right to resist forced entry into your house by the relatives to whom the house was mortgaged. Now that you have been forced to go out of your house, you can lodge a complaint against the intruders into your house for a case of trespass. You can also complain against your husband for opening a joint account through a forged signature and taking away your money. You can take up the case against the bank also for not exercising due diligence. A separate case of forgery for getting a Special Power of Attorney can also be taken up.

Q: My husband was working in a jewellery store as their Sales Manager. He had difference of opinion with the shop owner and wanted to leave his job. When he sent his resignation letter, the shop owner did not accept it. On the other hand he has filed a case of misappropriation against my husband and police have arrested my husband. What should I do?

—Vidya

A: Unless and until it is established that property belonging to the shop owner was entrusted to your husband and the said property went missing, it cannot be said that misappropriation has taken place. Let your husband find out whether any stock verification

was done and if the jewellery was missing when did it actually go missing. Unless these are established, it is difficult to prove a case of misappropriation. Now that your husband is arrested you have to get him out on bail. Please approach a competent criminal lawyer. If your husband is innocent, it is difficult to proceed with the case.

Q: I am working as a teacher in an institution. In the profile of our institution I have an orkut account. Some one has hacked into my account and has altered my profile and has written bad things about me. What should I do?

—Swarna

A: This is an offence under IT Act. Please lodge a complaint in the jurisdictional police station.

Q: I read an advertisement in a local newspaper stating that loans would be given at low interest rates. I contacted the advertiser and requested for a loan of Rs.30 lakhs. He asked me to provide photocopies of some documents which I provided. He in return contacted me and said that the loan has been sanctioned to me and that before disbursing the loan I need to pay Rs. 1.38 lakhs to a bank account. I deposited this money in the said account. Subsequently when the loan was not disbursed I tried to contact the advertiser but he has switched off his mobile phone. I don't know what to do?

—Rakesh

A: It is surprising that purely on the basis of a newspaper advertisement and phone call and without meeting the advertiser face to face, you were foolish enough to deposit money into some bank account. It is most likely that the account in question would have been closed. You may however lodge a complaint with the jurisdictional police for a case of cheating.

Q: Many of my friends got e-mail purportedly sent by me stating that I am in London and that my pocket was picked and I am in dire need of money. The e-mail also gave a bank account to which my friends were asked to remit the money. Is this not some type of e-mail hacking?

—T. Chandrashekar

A: It is definitely hacking of your e-mail account and sending messages to all persons who are in your contact list. A number of persons who receive such mails normally ignore the request but some do send money to the account mentioned. Usually the senders of such e-mails are residing in a foreign country and to bring them to book is difficult. It is always advisable not to respond to such distress e-mails. If such e-mail is received it is better to verify from the person concerned whether actually he has been a victim of any crime.

Q: I am an unmarried lecturer working in a college far away from my home town. I get lot of blank calls on my landline number. I am very scared. Can I lodge a complaint in a police station?

—Sunanda. H.

A: You may lodge a complaint with BSNL authorities who would be able to find out from which number you are getting blank calls in the night. You may also install a caller ID to your phone. Once you ascertain the identity of the caller, you may lodge a complaint with the local police.

Q: Can police add, delete or amend any section in the FIR while submitting chargesheet? If so under what provisions of law they can do it?

—Ram Vasanth

A: Chapter 12 of the Criminal Procedure Code deals with investigation of cognizable offences and filing reports

after completion of investigation with the Magistrate. As per the provisions contained thereon police is bound to register any complaint which discloses cognizable offence. After the case is registered it is incumbant on the police to investigate the complaint. During the course of the investigation the Investigating Officer may learn that (a) the complaint is totally false and has no substance; (b) the complaint is an exaggerated one and that in the complaint a minor offence is shown as a major one and (c) that the case is a civil or non-cognizable in nature. For example a police station may receive a complaint that 7 people entered into the house of the complainant, gagged his mouth and took away his wrist watch and gold chain. This complaint discloses an offence of dacoity and hence an FIR for dacoity will be registered. During the course of the investigation the Investigating Officer may find out that no such incident has taken place and the complaint is false. He may also learn that actually two people came to the complainant's house and picked up a quarrel with him and during this scuffle took away the watch and the chain. This will make it a case of robbery and not dacoity. During the investigation, police may also find that it is a fact that there was an alteration between the complainant and the accused and the accused who were only 2 persons merely hit the complainant with a stick and did not take away the watch or chain. If this fact comes to light no offence of robbery is made out but only an offence of hurt is made out. If the police find that the accused merely hit the complainant with their hands and not using any stick, then the case will be a simple hurt case which can be a non-cognizable case. Hence the contents of the FIR have to be verified by the IO and after his investigation whatever is the offence that is made out during investigation the related section of law is inserted. Hence Investigating Officer can add,

delete or amend the section of law in the FIR while filing the chargesheet in the Court.

Q: My wife's family is having a dispute with me; my wife has also joined them. They are all threatening to file a case of dowry harassment against me under section 498(a) of the IPC. How can I prevent this?

—Rajesh Menon

A: For a case under 498(a) to be filed it must be established that the husband or relatives of the husband of a woman has subjected the woman to cruelty. Cruelty means any wilful conduct which would drive the woman to commit suicide or to cause grave injury to her or harassment of the woman with a view to coerce her or her relatives to meet any unlawful demand of property. For this section to be attracted, your wife has to prove that you have subjected her for cruelty and she should provide evidence to show that. Anyone can register an FIR. If your wife or her relatives are unable to prove that you have harassed her, police can take up a case against them for falsely implicating you in a criminal case.

Q: Are there any separate section of law which can be used against employees of private firms when they commit fraud or cheating to the employer?

—Vipul Jain

A: If an employee of any firm has been entrusted with property dishonestly misappropriates such property, he can be punished for an offence of criminal breach of trust. If that person is a public servant or if he is a banker, merchant or an agent he can be prosecuted under section 409 IPC for which punishment is 10 years jail term. If any person commits cheating with the knowledge that wrongful loss will happen to the person whose interest he is bound to protect. [in this case the employer] section 418 of the IPC is attracted.

Q: My husband was arrested by the police and that when he was produced before the magistrate, police asked the magistrate for police custody. What is meant by Police Custody?

—Veena Shyam Sundar

A: A person who is arrested by the police has to be produced before a magistrate within 24 hours of his arrest. The police may need to interrogate the arrested person. Hence they seek Courts approval to take the person into their custody. This is called police custody. Normally police custody does not last more than 10 days. After investigation is over the police return the arrested person to the magistrate. When this happens the magistrate can grant the arrestee bail. However if the charge against the arrestee is non bailable, like that of murder the arrested person is sent to jail. This is called judicial custody. In simple words being in the police lock up is police custody and being in jail is judicial custody. It may also be clarified here that judicial custody means being in prison before and during trial.

Q: Is there any time limit to register an FIR? If a complaint is lodged in a police station for an offence under section 420 within how many hours should the FIR to be issued?

—Ratan Joshi

A: Whenever a complaint of a cognizable offence [section 420 is a cognizable offence] is received in a police station an FIR has to be registered immediately and Investigating Officer is bound to visit the scene of offence at the earliest. If police refuses to take up an FIR, the complainant can approach the Superintendent of Police or the Commissioner of Police or the Court for redressing his grievances.

Q: I suspect that my phone is being tapped. Are there any rules formed in this regard?

A: Phones can be tapped by government or its authorized officers as per Section 5 of the Indian Telegraph Act 1885. Rules regarding interception have been formed and as per Sec. 419 of Indian Telegraph Rules 1951, elaborate instructions have been given regarding telephone tapping. Adequate safeguards are provided to protect a citizen's privacy.

Q: My neighbour has partially encroached a site and is illegally constructing a building there. Can't the police stop this construction?

—Deepak Advani

A: If the person who possesses or owns the private property in question gives a complaint of illegal construction, definitely police can act. If the property is a public property, concerned government/municipal departments should lodge a complaint and the police will definitely take action.

Q: One of my employees has stolen data relating to my customers from my computer with an intention to sell them to my rivals. Can I take up this matter with the police?

—Vikas Bharadwaj

A: Theft of data from computers is definitely covered under Information Technology Act. Any person who does any dishonest or fraudulent act will be punishable under Sec. 66. Hence your employee can be booked for an offence under this act. Any person who receives such stolen information from your employee is also liable for punishment.

Q: In my locality, municipality is supplying very low quality water which is harmful to our health. Can I give complaint to the police against the municipal authorities for supplying unsafe drinking water?

—Vivek

A: For an act to be made out as criminal offence there must be an intention to cause wrongful laws or damage to the public. If there is deliberate intention to supply unsafe water, a case can be taken up against the concerned. As per Sec. 277 of IPC if any person voluntarily fouls the water of any reservoir so as to render it unfit for human consumption, he can be imprisoned for a term extending to 3 months. This is a cognizable offence and police can take up case directly. One has to establish that the act of the Municipality is international.

Q: When can the police enter a citizen's home? There are reports in the papers where cops have barged into houses where loud music was being played, confiscating the audio system and detaining people. My question basically is whether the police is authorized to enter a home without a warrant? If yes, under what circumstances can they do it and under what circumstances shouldn't they?

—Roshan

A: Police can enter any premises, for the purposes of search and arrest. If there is a suspicion that a cognizable offence is taking place or evidence relating to any under investigation is available in that premises, police can enter the premises, even by using force. It is not possible to take search warrants all the time as it is likely that the suspected person or suspected evidence can be removed if delay is caused. However while searching any premises; two witnesses are kept with the police party.

Q: We have complained to police against a religious institution situated in a residential premises. Their religious activity starts from 6 am and goes on till night. Their activities - chanting and shouting loudly using musical instruments, dancing, clapping etc - has affected our daily lives seriously. In spite of police

warning, they are not obeying and obliging. Kindly inform us regarding what steps to be taken according to law.

—Karthik

A: Under the Noise Pollution Regulation and Control Rules 2000, action can be taken against the institution in question. Please complain to Karnataka State Pollution Control Board. Under the Karnataka Police Act, a police officer can direct the concerned to reduce the nuisance caused. If the direction of the police is disobeyed, the concerned can be fined and even imprisoned.

Q: I have filed a case for divorce from my wife. We have been married for 10 months. She has filed 2 cases against me and my family, one under Sec 498 & 34 of Dowry Prohibition Act (for which the police have filed a B report), the second is a maintenance case. Her brother has sent an SMS to me and my friends wherein he has threatened to kill me. Is there any way I can take some action?

—Abhishek

A: The act of your brother-in-law amounts to Criminal intimidation which is punishable under Section 506 of the Indian Penal Code. The punishment for this section is seven-year jail term. You have to prove that the SMS originated only from your brother-in-law, as anyone could have sent an SMS in your brother-in-law's name. You can approach the jurisdictional Police Station after making sure of the origin of the SMS.

Q: Sir, it is observed that some officers trapped by the Lokayukta are reinstated. The Official Secrets Act is a good instrument as it is signed by all officials that they must declare their assets (movable/immovable) every year helping the investigating agency to come to a conclusion. Kindly elucidate.

—Pednekar Vasant

A: Any government servant involved in a criminal case is normally placed under suspension and during the period of suspension he gets subsistence allowance. The longer the suspension period, the higher the allowance. Official Secrets Act has nothing to do with suspension. All government servants are expected to file their property returns annually. The investigators in Lokayukta can access these files.

Q: Most police chiefs complain about shortage of staff. What is the magnitude of shortage of officers and constables in Karnataka? What steps is the police taking to fill that shortage given the fact that terrorism is a major threat to our country now?

—Hasan

A: There is tremendous shortage of police staff in almost all states. In Karnataka, the shortage is of about 10,000 personnel. The State Police has taken up steps to fill up the vacancies. In the last three years 13,000 personnel have been recruited. The process of recruiting 400 PSIs is already on.

Q: Whether one likes it or not, the general perception of police is that it is 'corrupt'. This is because some police personnel do not follow the rules themselves. Why do high ranking police officers fail to do justice to their job under political intervention? What are your views and suggestions on this?

—CM Ponnappan, Mysore

A: The image that the police is corrupt, brutal, unethical and that it does not follow law is an outcome of police being a much closed organization. Members of public rarely interact with police. They go to a police station only if they become victims of crime. At best their brush with police is only on the streets. Because of this, public rarely comes across the positive traits of the police and they don't even know under what difficult circumstances police function. The MIT of US conducted

an experiment in Rajasthan recently where groups of public regularly visited police stations as "observers". Their perception of the police changed radically! Like in any other organization, there are black sheep within the police and they need to be weeded out. Corruption can be minimized if the members of public resolve not to give bribes and to report about persons who demand bribes. I don't agree that high ranking police officers are not doing anything to curb corruption. Constant upgradation of professional skills, a good system of rewards and punishments, better working conditions, better salary etc will go a long way in changing the police system. The Police Reforms, which the Supreme Court has mandated will help the organization fare better in future.

Q: What is the checklist to be followed by police before taking any person into custody? What is the procedure to be followed in case of arrest in cognizable and non-cognisable cases in view of recent amendments to CrPC? If a cop on the street asks me to go to police station, can I refuse? What are my rights?

—Pradeep D.

A: If a non-cognizable case is committed in the presence of a police officer, arrest can be made without a warrant, if the accused refuses to give his name and address to the police officer. (S 42 Cr.PC). A police officer investigating a crime can require the attendance of any person before him and such person shall attend (S.160 Cr.PC). Therefore, if you are called by the police through a written notice, please obey the memo. An arrested person is required to be produced before a Magistrate within 24 hours of his arrest and there shall be no infringement of the human rights of the arrestee. Regarding the amendment of Cr.PC about the procedure to be followed after arrest, the police officer should be satisfied that the arrest is necessary, and while making arrest he should wear his name plate, he should prepare

a memo of arrest to be attested by a family member or a respectable person of the locality, and the arrestee to be told the grounds of arrest. The arrestee is entitled to keep a lawyer of his choice during interrogation and medical check up to be made immediately after arrest. Persons accused of committing offences for which punishment is less than seven-year jail term will not be arrested easily as per the amendment.

Q: Sir, I have been fooled and made to remit so much money to some two accounts in ICICI Bank branch Delhi and I have lodged a complaint with Mangalore Pandeshwara Police Station and District Crime Branch Inspector had enquired about the same case. What action can be taken in this regard?

—Suryanarayan, Mangalore

A: You must have become a victim of what is popularly known as the Nigerian fraud. Normally fraudsters send emails saying that you have inherited huge sums of money or you have won a lottery and ask you to pay a processing fee to some blank accounts in India to claim the full amount. After making you pay thousands of rupees, the fraudster vanishes! The Kerala police have arrested a Nigerian in a similar case and probably your case may be detected. Please ask Pandeshwar Police to get in touch with Crime Branch, CID, Kerala.

Q: How we can file a FIR? Where we can file it? What are the procedures of CrPC?

—Prashant Wajantri

A: FIRs reporting occurrence of a cognizable offence can be filed by visiting the jurisdictional or any police station. The report can be sent by post, and sometimes even by e-mail. It can be reported orally through telephone. Reports regarding cognizable offences can be filed in Courts, Office of the Commissioner or Superintendent of Police, or a police station. Sec. 154 Cr.PC gives details regarding FIR.

Q: Sir I am from a middle class family. I have let out my residential premises to a person who has defaulted in paying rent. Now he has mortgaged it to another person, on enquiry he behaves very rudely. What help can I get from the police in this matter?

—Saravana, Bangalore

A: The problem you are facing does not come under the purview of Criminal Law and you have to approach a civil court through a lawyer and get your grievance redressed. At best the police may call your tenant and advise him not to behave rudely with you.

Q: On Bangalore Roads one comes across at least one auto that is pumping pollutants into the air every 100 m. Are there no norms against pollution and why isn't the police catching these people for this? Is there a mafia that sells polluted fuel?

—Pushkar Talwalkar

A: Any polluting vehicle can definitely be booked. Three agencies, namely, the Police, the Transport Department and the Pollution Control Board can take action. The City Traffic Police has a heavy workload and most of its time is spent towards regulation of traffic. We need more officers and men for strict enforcement of laws. With more and more autos going in for LPG fuel, the air pollution levels could come down. In New Delhi, Public Transport Vehicles compulsorily use CNG, due to which pollution levels have come down. Such a policy could help us in Bangalore.

Q: I was wondering that if cops can use force to enter a house and search if they have information of a cognizable offence occurring at the checks and balances that are in place to ensure cops do not misuse this power? If a cop enters my house, what are my rights as a citizen?

—Roshan

A: Two respectable citizens of the locality are to be present as witnesses with the police whenever they search any premises. Before conducting a search, the police party must get themselves subjected to search so that no one can allege that the police planted incriminating material during search operations. Search panchnama should be drawn in the presence of inmates of the house where the search is conducted. A seizure list of all properties seized shall be prepared and a copy of it shall be given to the inmates. Proper care should be taken if only women are present on the premises. It is prudent to involve women police officers/women witnesses for such searches. Decency and decorum needs to be ensured. Nowadays, search parties videograph important search. If the police come to your house for search, you can ask them if they have a search warrant and if there is one, affix your signature on it. You can ask the names and designation of the officers and ask them to show their identity cards. You can ask them the purpose of their search.

Q: I am a graduate and want to get into the police force, but I have come across a number of media reports showing that the police personnel, specially women, face a lot of harassment. Does the department have a separate cell to tackle such complaints?

—Parimala, Belgaum

A: A number of women graduates are working with the Karnataka Police. Their rank ranges from DGP to constable. Ten per cent of police jobs in the rank of constable and PSIs are reserved for women in our state and in general women in our Department are happy. I have got surveys conducted in two districts of Karnataka to find out whether women police face any harassment from their male colleagues. A majority of them had no complaints. As per the orders of the Supreme Court in

Visaka Case, committees to look into complaints of harassment of women at work place have been constituted.

Q: A female colleague of mine used to receive troublesome messages and e-mails from a senior colleague who continued to send them despite constant warnings. When she reported this to the higher ups, the issue was brushed off by the department, stating that they were not harmful and asked her to resign from the post if she had such problems and the person she had complained was in a senior post. In such a situation, can the police come for help?

—Nagesh, Dharwad

A: Your friend should complain to the jurisdictional police about the harassment by her seniors, by showing copies of the SMSs e-mails etc. Police would definitely help her.

Q: The Supreme Court of India has banned the use of loudspeakers all over India from 10 pm to 6 am. The Supreme Court has also provided detailed guidelines for use of loudspeakers. Surprisingly, the police department which is vested with the responsibility of permitting use of loud speakers is not monitoring or controlling the use of loudspeakers. I have complained to all officers concerned including the Karnataka State Pollution Control Board. But there has been no action in this regard. What can the police department do to uphold the law of the land and ensure quiet for peace-loving citizens? What else should I do to make police department implement the orders of Supreme Court of India as regards noise pollution?

—A Bhanu, Bangalore

A: Why don't you approach the Commissioner of Police, Bangalore City or the DG&IGP, Karnataka State, or the Chairman Karnataka Pollution Control Board?

You could also consider filing a writ petition in the High Court.

Q: A group of local persons (land mafia) schemed to blackmail the site owners of an extension formed about 80 years back by the municipality by acquiring lands. The group systematically knocked off records from record rooms of city municipality, taluk office, Asst Commissioner's office and even sub registrar's office. They even managed to get stay orders in court against two site owners who had started construction of building by creating bogus 'Pahani' (record of rites) and succeeded in black mailing one person. Now all are totally exposed in number of RTI disclosures and court cases. The black mailers have pilfered Govt. records of permanent nature, created false records and false evidences and witnesses and conceded evidence to gain. We want to seek help of Police to book the blackmailers. Please guide us.

—DN Jayaram, Tumkur

A: If you are in possession of evidence to support your allegation, please approach the Superintendent of Police, Tumkur who will definitely help you.

Q: Air pollution due to smoke belching autos, lorries and buses deserves more attention from your dept than now. The air pollution affects all citizens of the city, particularly your traffic policemen whom you are heading as a family head. Instead of wasting present manpower on things like catching two wheelers throughout the month for minor offences like emission test that is just a few days old, insurance not renewed etc, your staff should pay more attention to air pollution. Please advise your staff not to bother about the private cars of later than 2000 year for emission test. They are normally in fit condition due to regular servicing.

Thus existing manpower can be utilized for better use. You can also authorize some good citizens of over 45 years to inform the police network the vehicle number.

—B V Rao

A: The traffic policemen who perform duty on city roads for 8 hours a day are heavily subjected to both Air and Sound Pollution. As it is there are not enough traffic policemen for regulation of traffic on Bangalore roads. Hence, enforcement of various act and rules related to motor vehicles is not getting the attention it deserves. Some citizens of Bangalore are helping the traffic police by volunteering to work as traffic wardens. When adequate numbers of traffic police men are in place, we can give more attention to polluting vehicles.

Q: Will you take the lead to avoid overlapping responsibility of Police, Transport Dept & PCB, which is counterproductive?

ii) Uniformed police officers instil more law obedience in the public. Will you please minimize public/TV appearances of police top brass in civilian clothing?

—K V Balachandran

A: I do not agree that overlapping of responsibilities in respect of pollution control is counter productive. Every department needs to pay adequate attention to pollution control so that together we can bring about a change.

All police officers are expected to be wearing uniform; only such personnel who are working in Intelligence and Crime Branches do not wear uniform for obvious reasons. I do agree with you that uniformed police men will instil obedience of law. I am sure all police personnel who are expected to wear uniform wear it while on official duty including senior officers.

Q: Recently I had lost my wallet; I have given complaint to nearby police station in Bangalore. After giving complaint the police officer asked me Rs. 20 to give to injured person sitting nearby. Is there any rule that I should give him as a fee?

—Shaiz C.

A: It is wrong on the part of policemen to ask you to pay some money to injured person. You are not bound to pay money for lodging any complaint. Police cannot force you to do philanthropy acts.

Q: I am an elderly person. The other day I requested an auto bearing number plate only in Kannada to take me to my doctor whose clinic is about six km away. But he refused to ply. I could not note the number as I could not read Kannada. Is carrying number plate only in local language permissible as per MVA. If someone is particular about his own language should he not have bilingual name plates? Suppose the driver is involved in an offence, how a person who does not know the local language makes a complaint to the police? Please clarify.

—P.S. Sukumaran

A: Every vehicle registered in India is supposed to have its number plates in English language and Roman numerals. However in certain places the vehicles display number plates in the local language. A new initiative of the Central Government to have uniform type of number plates across the country is likely to be put in place shortly. If this happens the difficulty you encountered will not happen.

Q: My neighbour keeps very late hours and all sorts of shady characters visit his home at all times. One day I complained about him to Hoysala and they came and warned him. Ever since he learnt that I have complained, he gesticulates at me and threatens me.

I informed about him to the local police over the phone, they did not act. Please advise.

—Surya Prakash

A: Even though your neighbour is intimidating you, his action does not fall into the category of a cognizable offence. In a cognizable case, police can register an FIR, arrest the accused without a warrant from the court and investigate the case. In a non-cognizable case police can investigate only after obtaining orders from a competent court. You are requested to approach the court through a lawyer and get your grievances redressed.

Q: In January, I had been to Malaysia and made payments for purchases done there through my credit card. When I received my monthly statement I found that I have been billed for purchases not made by me. I raised a dispute with my bank regarding this, but so far it has not been resolved. Can I lodge an FIR against the card issuing bank?

—Anant, Bangalore

A: Obviously some fraudster in Malaysia has copied the information contained in the magnetic tape of your credit card, duplicated the same and has used it to purchase some goods. After you returned from abroad, you should have informed the bank about the purchases made and the date of your return to India, so they could block payments to merchant establishments abroad. Certain banks issue their customers new cards, the moment they return from North East Asian countries. From August 1 of this year, all card holders get an SMS alert the moment purchases above Rs 5,000 is made on their card. You cannot lodge an FIR against the bank.

Q: I was in my car parked on a street around 10 pm with a friend having beer. After an hour's time, a constable

walked by and asked us to leave as it was 11 pm. We weren't nuisance for anybody and hadn't caused trouble. His contention was that it was a VIP area and I couldn't park there. When I told him there was no 'No Parking' sign, he got offended and said that he had doubts on why we were there. He used his cell phone to call for a Hoysala jeep. We left after that as we didn't want any further trouble and weren't sure what our rights were in such a situation. Why is it that cops act as private security guards for the rich and the powerful while they treat others as second class citizens? I'd like to know if the cop was within his right to chase us off. Can't we stay on our streets past 11 pm? In such situations, what action can cops take and under what laws? What are our rights as citizens?

—Roshan R Krishnan

A: Please put yourself in the shoes of the constable. He sees a parked car in the night on a street through which VIPs (in other words, persons who are under security threat) pass by. There are two persons in the car having drinks. He does not know whether the occupants of the car are robbers or terrorists or kidnappers or persons whose intention is to cause damage. He does not know whether they are armed or unarmed. He does not know whether the boot of the car contains explosives or weapons. Since a public road is not a home or a pub or a bar where people can drink and make merry, the constable did the correct thing by calling for help. It is not correct to say that police work as private security guards for the rich and powerful. Imagine what would happen to society if there were no policemen for more than 24 hours in a city like ours. Police ensure safety and security of each citizen. That is why the cop in question got suspicious about you. Instead of you being in the car, if there were a couple of underworld dons or terrorists in the car and if they had thrown bombs or if they

had kidnapped a girl living in that locality, what would your comments be about the police? Thousands of persons use our streets beyond 11 pm. If action of any citizen arouses suspicion, it is for the citizen to prove that he is innocent.

Q: How can we bridge the gap between the citizens and the police? There is a feeling that the police do not hear citizen's views objectively and do what they want. Don't you feel that there is an urgent need for implementation of police reforms?

—N. Mukund

A: Police cannot achieve anything. Police also need to learn that they are here to serve the people. All successful police leaders have understood this and have involved the citizenry in the police work. I do agree with you that some police officers do not hear the views of others. The training schools are now training policemen to behave and act differently. There is definitely an urgent need for police reforms, and I am happy to state that we in Karnataka have already implemented two of the six reforms.

Q: If a person is taken to the station, is it arrest or detention? If a person is asked to come to station on some charge which is non-cognizable and which was done months ago and for which no complaint was lodged (eg nuisance cases), is the person obligated to accompany the constable to station even after he has given his address. Can a constable check my bag without my permission anywhere on the street?

Can a constable act outside of his jurisdiction in case of non-cognizable cases? Can a woman be taken to station in non-cognizable cases and what are her rights? Can a woman be picked up on charges of indecent behaviour, obscenity or is a warrant necessary? Can a woman be picked up from lodge if she is with her boyfriend on charge of prostitution or

is a warrant necessary? If a lodge refuses to give room to a couple who are not married, whom can I complain to? Basically, under what conditions can a person be picked up without warrant and when he can't be arrested?

—Pradeep D.

A: Taking a person to a police station does not mean arrest or detention. Persons are routinely called to the station for enquiry into petitions, to record statements in cases under investigation etc. If a police officer is investigating into a non-cog case, can he not call the accused and enquire? If a police officer has suspicion that some stolen article is being carried in your bag, he has a right to check it even on the street. A woman can be picked up by police if she is indulging in indecent behaviour in public. However, she will not be detained in the police station from dusk to dawn and she will be searched only by a woman police officer. The code of criminal procedure is now being amended and many provisions relating to arrest are being modified. A lodging house can refuse to give a room to even married couple. How can you complain against that?

Q: A man crossing a road is knocked down by a vehicle in an accident. How does police take action?

—Emani J Hari Kiran.

A: A criminal case is registered about the accident. The victim is taken to a hospital and given treatment. Police will take action against the driver of the vehicle if he drove the vehicle in a rash and negligent manner.

Q: I received a notice from the Bangalore city traffic police to pay a fine of Rs. 100, stating that my vehicle had jumped traffic signal at Jalahalli Cross on 20.03.08 at 18.53 hrs. I paid the fine at Rajajinagar Traffic Police Station because I was worried about a brush with the

law. However, I wrote them a letter stating that I paid the fine under protest for the following reasons: The notice states that my vehicle is a "motorcycle" but I do not own a motorcycle at all. 2) Being a senior citizen, I ride very less mostly in the mornings around Rajajinagar and nearby. In the afternoon and evenings I stay indoors only. There is no chance at all my riding the vehicle at Jalahalli Cross, that too in the evenings. It is a mystery how my vehicle number was recorded there. There could have been a mistake while noting down the vehicle number. I requested the traffic police station to send proof of having noticed my vehicle there. The letter was acknowledged by the Department on 30.05.08 but I have not received a reply.

—Gopalakrishna Shroff

A: The City traffic police have installed surveillance cameras at several points in Bangalore and these cameras record traffic violations by motor vehicles. Apart from this traffic constables located at various traffic points note down violations in specially designed proforma given to them. Later on, the registration number of the offending vehicle is fed to a computer through which the ownership particulars of the vehicle are obtained and fine notices are sent to the registered owners. In your question you seem to admit that you own a vehicle but sparingly ride it. Do you own a two-wheeler and does the registration number of your vehicle tally with the number in the police notice? Did you allow anyone to use your vehicle on the date mentioned? There might also have been a mistake on the part of the person who read the registration number wrongly. You could have raised a dispute after receiving the notice. You should have addressed the letter to City Traffic Police, 13th floor Public Utility Building, M.G. Road, Bangalore. Now that the incident is more than 18 months old it is difficult to verify it.

Q: After one week of the Ganesha Festival, a group of people erected a pandal near my place which falls under Thyagarajanagar police station and put huge speakers and loud music. When we complained to the police station they hung up saying they have taken permission till 10.30 pm, whereas the rule is till 10 pm only. There was a van standing and when complaint was given to them they just smiled and asked us to enjoy the event. I complained to the control room too and they said they can't do anything. There is a hospital on this road but still they got the permission. We were even told that if we pay some money action will be taken against the group. Can anything be done about the poeple in this police station?

—Smitha Rajakumar

A: Normally use of loudspeakers in public places is not permitted beyond 10 pm. I am given to understand that consequent to the representation made by certain State Governments, the Supreme Court has given some relaxation for use of loudspeakers beyond 10 pm during some festivals. Under Sec 37 of the Karnataka Police Act, the volume of the speakers in any public place should not be at such a pitch as to be audible beyond 200 feet from where the loudspeaker is installed. You should complain to the Bangalore Police Commissioner regarding the demand of bribe by the Police. Please also lodge a complaint with the Lokayukta.

Q: Earlier it was CoD and now CID. What is the difference between the two? Is the CID the same organization and just an agency which investigates cases referred by the government?

—Santhosh Kumar

A: Corps of Detectives, created in 1974 by the State Government is part of the Criminal Investigation Department (CID). Since there is no concept of the

CoD in other states, officers of Karnataka had to explain their duties to police officers of other states whenever they went out for investigation. Hence it was decided to use the term CID. CID which is a part of the State Police takes up for investigation all cases of custodial death, all cases of dowry deaths, and all cases referred by the Government and the State Police Chief.

Q: Now-a-day's cases of lock up deaths are occurring very frequently in our state. What is the reason?

—Lokanath Reddy, Kolar

A: Contrary to your perception deaths in custody in Karnataka over the years have come down. This is because policemen at all levels are trained to respect human rights and any human rights violation is viewed seriously. The Karnataka State has an office with a rank of IG to oversee human rights enforcements. The State Human Rights Commission and the National Human Rights Commission are also very active and have become strong deterrent in curbing custodial violence. Police officers who willfully violate human rights are punished. With NGOs also becoming very active in exposing human rights violation on the part of police, the cases of custodial violence have come down.

Q: Private jeeps and maxi cabs are always over-loaded. Auto rickshaws carry 10-12 kids to and from schools endangering their lives. Can police stop this?

—R.B. Pawar

A: Every public transport vehicle has to adhere to its licensed seating capacity. Overloaded transport vehicles always endanger lives. It is the duty of the Transport Department and Police to book such vehicles. Courts have also come out strongly against auto rickshaws carrying a large number of school

children. Please approach the SP and RTC of your district and request them to take action.

Q: It is often said that the police experience difficulty in getting witnesses to support its case. Why is that so?

—A.C. Sadashiva

A: It is a fact that many of our citizens are afraid to report cases they actually witness to the police for the fear that they would be asked to come to courts for deposing their evidence. Normally, criminal cases take a very long time to conclude and witnesses feel that they would be asked to go to courts again and again thereby wasting their precious time. Actually witnesses are given TA and DA to appear before courts and give their evidence. The public prosecutor can be approached so that the evidence of the concerned witness can be taken up in a quick manner. Because of not getting witness to depose in criminal cases, many end in acquittal. Only a strong social sense among citizens will change this state of affairs.

Q: It is observed that police officers are behaving more like politicians. They listen more to their political bosses than to their own superiors. What is being done to curb this?

—G.S. Nagesh

A: The Supreme Court has ordered a wide variety of reforms in the Police department which if implemented, will go a long way in curbing the tendency you have described on the part of some officers. Our Government has already constituted the Police Establishment Board, as well as the State Security Commission which makes the police more accountable.

Q: I have a salary account in a leading private sector bank at Bangalore. A few days ago I discovered that

somebody hacked into my account and has transferred Rs. 75,000/- to his account. I am perplexed, please help me.

—S. Gurudev

A: You have been a victim of Internet banking fraudsters. You must have un-wittingly given your log-in and password details of your account in reply to an e-mail purportedly sent by the bank or you might have shared these details with somebody else. No person should disclose his log-in and password details to any one. No bank official can ask you for these details. You should keep changing your password frequently. Your password should contain both alphabets and numbers. You should have asked your bank to block all money transfers through internet. You should have asked your bank to send you SMS the moment the transaction of more than Rs. 5,000/- was made through your account. If you had to transfer money urgently, you could have done it through RTGS. Now-a-days for money transfer through internet some banks have added extra security measures. You can lodge a complaint regarding hacking your account in the Cyber Police Station situated at CID Headquarters. Bringing the offenders of such crimes to book is quite difficult as the perpetrators are usually sitting abroad.

Q: I am a graduate. I want to join as Sub-Inspector in Karnataka Police. How do I go about it?

—V.K. Puttaswamy, Hassan

A: Recently the state police have advertised for recruitment of Police Sub-Inspectors–Civil. To be eligible, the candidate must be 21-26 years of age [28 for SC/ST, OBC] and a graduate. Applicant's minimum height should be 170 cms [157 cms for women], chest 81-86 cms [not for women], and weight 45 kgs. (for women only). The candidate should undergo a Physical Endurance Test comprising of 1600mtrs run in 7 min

[400mtrs in 2 min for women] long jump of not less than 3.80mtrs [2.50 for women] high jump of not less than 1.2mtrs [0.90 for women] and shot put. Candidates who qualify the Physical Endurance Test will be put through a written exam comprising of two papers and those who qualify will be put through a viva-voce test. Candidates clearing all the above will be medically examined and select list published.

Q: My scooter was recently stolen in Mysore City. When I went to lodge a complaint, the police officers asked me to come a week later. I went after 1 week and they reluctantly registered the case. Now it is more than 3 months since the two-wheeler is lost. The police are not giving me any information about the progress.

—Srikar. R.

A: Now-a-days a large number of two-wheelers are being stolen in our cities and towns. In the year 2008 more than 8,000 vehicles have been stolen in the State. Many a time the stolen vehicles are transported to other states and are sold. Many other times the vehicle is stripped down and the spare parts are sold as junk separately. It is reported that one can buy a stolen two-wheeler for as low as Rs. 5,000/-. Hence detection of motor vehicle theft case is very difficult indeed. It is therefore, quite likely that you may not get your two-wheeler back. You may request the Investigating Officer to submit a final report in the court stating that the case is undetected. Based on the report you may think of claiming Insurance. The police should have registered the case the moment you approached them. If at all you buy a new vehicle please install safety features. You might lock the wheel of your two-wheeler or use extra locks for your handle.

Q: My niece Hema aged 16 years is missing from her home. We searched for her for 2 days and when we

did not get any clue, we approached jurisdictional Police Station. The Head Constable at the station did not receive our complaint and asked us to search for the missing girl for one more week and then come back. When we went back after one week, he asked us to bring photographs and other descriptive particulars. He also asked us that the Police have to print pamphlets describing the missing girl and asked us to pay Rs. 1,000 as printing charges. We paid the same, but till today Hema has not returned, we are worried.

—Smt. Suma Prakash

A: Normally girls of Hema's age group run away from home to become TV or movie stars or elope with their boy friends whom they intend to marry. Some girls are enticed by bad elements into escaping from home and these girls end up in brothels. In our state, whenever complaint about a missing person is received, police are bound to register a case and give copy of the complaint to the complainant. Once the missing complaint is received the police normally flash the particulars of the missing person to all the neighbouring Police Stations, and information is also given to neighbouring states. Unclaimed and unidentified dead bodies found in the vicinity are also checked. The details of the missing persons are put in Police web site and efforts are made to trace them. If the girl has run away on her own she would definitely be found. However, if the girl is trafficked, it is difficult to detect the case early. Only when Police raid brothels and rescue girls, such cases are detected. If Hema is so far has not been traced, you may once again approach the SP of the concerned district to make more efforts in tracing her. The success in such cases is quite low indeed.

Q: A person caught by the police is made to be released on bail by politicians. If the accused escapes after release what will you do?

—Balaiah

A: An arrested person is entitled to be released on bail either by the Police or Court. It depends on the offence committed by him. As you say, arrested persons are not released on the advice of politicians. Before releasing a person on bail adequate surety and security is taken. If the person still absconds there are many ways to compel his appearance. Surely very few people abscond after getting released on bail.

Q: I have a threat to my life and hence want to purchase a revolver. How should I go about it?

—Ramarathnam, Bangalore

A: In order to obtain a weapon license you must satisfy the Licensing Authority (in your case the Commissioner of Police, Bangalore City) the need to have a weapon. The application should be made in the prescribed proforma and fee for the same need to be paid. A simple verification is done by the Police Authority and if they feel the need for you to have a license you will be granted a license. The weapon license can be limited to the area of Bangalore city or can have a State wide jurisdiction. After obtaining license you are expected to purchase a weapon and produce the weapon before Licensing Authority. License needs to be renewed from time to time. Now today's small weapons made in foreign countries are quite expensive. We in India are also making small weapons which are cost effective.

Q: Recently my neighbour has given his vehicle garage on rent to a motor mechanic; because of this a lot of nuisance is being caused to us. The mechanic does tinkering job also and there is too much of noise pollution. Can we approach the Police?

—Nanjundeshwar, Davanagere

A: Yours is a very common problem. Many residential areas are now being used for commercial purposes. You can approach the Municipal Authorities to redress your

grievances. You can also approach the jurisdictional police regarding noise pollution.

Q: Sir, I am a student from Udupi. We have a lot of private buses plying with "express" board on them. These buses use vacuum horns with very high sound which is more than anyone can tolerate and drive on a very high speed. I myself had pain on my eardrum due to this several times. Neither the police nor the RTO is taking any action on them even if they blow such horn in front of their office/jeep/ or SP's car. My question is "Is the police/ RTO not empowered to stop such violations? Who is the proper authority to control such violations? What can be done to stop such violations?

—Mukesh Naik

A: Using shrill horns is prohibited; it is the Transport Department which has to tackle such violations. Over speeding has to be tackled by the Jurisdictional Police. I am surprised that the local authorities are turning a blind eye to such violations. You may please write to the SP, Udupi for needful action. I will also separately inform him.

Q: I was a witness in a rioting case which happened in front of my house. Police have taken my statement and I have been asked to appear as a prosecution witness. The opposite party is asking me not to depose against them. And they are threatening me and my family. What is to be done?

—B.A. Bhoslay, Raichur

A: Please approach the concerned Police Station immediately and explain to them about the threat. You should also inform the court. Adequate protection will be given to you by the concerned. You need not fear to tell the truth and don't get cowed down by any threat.

Q: When I was browsing a footpath book stall on Avenue Road, a person appeared suddenly and started demanding money from the street vendor. The vendor helplessly pleaded that there was no business on that day and he didn't earn a single pie. The fellow departed with a stern warning that he should get the amount next day with arrears. On enquiry the vendor tells me that he has to pay mamool to local rowdies for selling books on that piece of footpath. Do you see any end to this and how?

—A Obireddy, Bangalore

A: What you have described has been happening in cities and towns since a very long time. This has continued because many a time the victims do not complain to the Police and silently pay the rowdies. In many cities there is an Anti Rowdy Squad which takes care of such rowdies.

Q: I am a middle class non-vegetarian bachelor employed in private sector. I find it difficult to get a house on rent all the time because I am a non-vegetarian, or because I am a bachelor or because I am from private sector as they prefer only government employees. Even when I manage to find one, the landlord refuses to give me a copy of rent agreement. Sometimes the rent for a small house is exorbitantly high. Isn't there a legal recourse to this exploitation by high rentals and discrimination on such frivolous grounds?

Also some landlords impose conditions that female colleagues of mine cannot visit me. Is it illegal for them to visit my house? Or is landlord permitted to impose these conditions. I find it ridiculous in this age and time when even live-in relationships is recognized by the state of Maharastra. Are live-in relationships illegal in Karnataka? Also previously one of my

landlords threw out my luggage in my absence as I had delayed that month's rent. Is this legal?

—Pradeep D.

A: The problems mentioned by you do not come under the purview of criminal law, except the action of throwing out your belongings from your home. If your landlord entered your home during your absence, his action amounts to house trespass and he can be criminally prosecuted.

Q: Thank you for responding to citizen concerns, however one could hardly see enforcements among officers at junior level. For example the Government has spent crores of rupees on BTRAC BOARDS, especially in Jayanagar, Bangalore, but in front of all the No Parking Boards vehicles are parked for hours together, what is the purpose of spending huge amount of money when there is no enforcement? Similarly, when we want to give certain general information in confidentiality (not complaints) the CONTROL ROOM asks for the identity. When it is public information useful to Police and to ascertain, why there is need for identity.

—M N Rao

A: The enforcement by traffic officials especially regarding action on vehicles parked in no parking zone is not really visible. Many a time, fine notices are sent to the owners of offending vehicles by post. Many a time, the vehicles are towed away and the owner is made to pay the fine as well as towing charges. In recent times, Bangalore Traffic Police have started a new system of locking the wheels of vehicles which are parked in no parking zones. If you want to give any confidential information to the police, you may talk to the concerned ACP/DCP instead of the control room. You need not disclose your identity to them.

Q: Sir, I am running a sawmill in Mysore. Last week one head constable from CID Forest Mobile Squad Mysore

came to my mill and demanded Rs 5000 for Dasehra Festival. He also said I should pay Rs 1000 every month which goes to his higher officer in the department. When I opposed he threatened me and took Rs 2000. Sir is it obligatory to pay the mamool to them? Please take appropriate action against the person and render me justice.

—Manoj Murthy

A: I do not understand as to why you have to pay bribes to Forest Mobile Squad officials. Why did you pay Rs 2000? If he approaches you again, please inform the SP or Lokayukta who is in Mysore and get a trap laid. You should not pay bribes to anyone. Meanwhile, please let me know the name of the person who approached you and I will take necessary action.

Q: I am working in a call center; I am in love with a girl studying in 9th standard. We both want to marry each other. Will there be any problem?

—M. Prakash

A: Since the girl is studying in 9th standard, it is presumed that she is less than 18 years of age. Even though, she is willing for marriage, if you take her away from her family to get married, you will have to face a case of kidnap and possibly of rape. You may wait till the girl gets to be of marriageable age.

Q: Some burglers entered my house and stole gold ornaments worth Rs. 1,00,000/-. Recently the police caught a thief and told that our case has been solved. When we went to collect the stolen goods, we were told that the goods recovered are only 50% of the goods stolen. Have the policemen misappropriated the recovered gold?

—Vishwesh

A: Detecting a property offence is time consuming. Out of 100 theft cases, only about 35 get detected. Many

a time the thief would have spent the property stolen. Supposing he has stolen cash from your home he will spend the same for his own entertainment. In such a case recovery is impossible. Many a time if he has stolen articles like VCR/TV etc., then recovery would be 100%. If gold ornaments are stolen the thief would have sold it to some receivers of stolen property and getting back the entire gold from the receiver is well nigh impossible as it is the word of the thief against the word of the receiver. It is therefore wrong to presume that the police have misappropriated your property.

Q: I am a senior citizen and I personally requested the Inspector of Police(traffic),Basavanagudi on 20th instant, to arrange to clear a pushcart vendor illegally occupying the footpath in front of my apartment selling fruit juice. I also followed it up with a letter for action that needed to be taken up on B.P.Wadia Road to ensure that the footpaths are exclusively kept for pedestrians. Our road is a small stretch of arterial road with very heavy traffic and the residents find it very difficult even to cross the road. Added to our woes is the illegal mushrooming of vendors on the footpaths on a permanent basis with their supposed to be moving pushcarts. Also many unscrupulous citizens park their cars and two wheelers on our footpath causing all the more inconvenience to pedestrians. I know the reasons for the police inaction and perhaps you too. I feel that my letter would have already been despatched by the police via the DUSTBIN. How do I make the police a bit more responsible?

– S.R.Venkataram

A: I do agree with you that encroachment of footpath has become a serious problem in Bangalore. City traffic police are doing other duty regularly but they cannot concentrate only on this problem since many other

serious problems keep cropping up. Often the footpath vendors approach the courts stating that their only means of livelihood is being snatched. Street vendors are not exclusive problem in Bangalore. It is a world wide phenomenal. It is necessary for us to dedicate some place for such vendors to earn their livelihood. Municipal Authority and the police can and should act in unisome to minimize such problems. Parking cars on footpaths should be locked into by the traffic police and only a concerted traffic by the police and awareness among the public can solve this.

Q. An inspector claiming from CBI, came asking for me in my office, most probably seeing my name plate outside my office. On asking what the matter was, he told me that he is looking for my neighbour, whose office was closed and then he asked me to come to his office. He claimed that my name is also their in my neighbours fraud document. I am sure I do not have any connection with my neighbour, what-so-ever. Please let me know, can he force me to go to his office for a case in which I do not have any connection.

– Ramesh Gupta

A: If any person approaches you claiming to be from the police or from enforcement agencies that you have to do is to ask for his identity card and ensure that he is a government official. If any govt. official asks you to visit him in his office, you can request him to give this in writing. If a police officer calls you to a police station as a witness in any case, he is supposed to give you a written notice. If you have doubts about any person's identity, you should always approach the higher-ups in the Dept and ascertain the truth.

Q: A couple of days ago, when I was standing at traffic signal in Chord Road, I was shocked to see eunuchs demanding money from motorists. But I was even

more shocked when one person came to me asking for money because I thought they trouble only men. Luckily I got a green signal and I sped away. I also noticed a motorist who first refused to give money, then gave money without bearing the embarrassment. So I request you to do something to save people from such situations. I know that there are many more important things to be dealt with and you might also say it's not a crime, but put yourself in such a situation where you don't have money when you are approached by a eunuch. Terrible!! Right? So kindly oblige.

—Sneha

A: Bangalore City Police have already tackled this problem. I have to recount here that when some policemen rounded up .... harassing pedestrian a big delegation went to the police top brass and complained that the unique were ill-treated. I also want to point out that when the Delhi High Court was hearing the case filed by an NGO regarding homosexuality being an offence. Some advocates complained to the Court about harassment meted out by the Bangalore Police to some .... and that sexual minorities were dealt with harshly. Any type of begging on the streets needs to be curbed and empower the police to deal with the problem. Unfortunately there is too less a number of police to tackle so many problems that confront society.

Q: A few months ago a friend of mine borrowed Rs. 50,000/- from me promising that he will return the same within 15 days. Despite my repeated requests, he is not returning the money. Can I approach the police?

—Ramakrishna

A: Your problem does not come under the purview of criminal law. You have to approach a Civil Court supposing the person who borrowed money from you

has given you post dated cheques and if any such cheques has bounced, you can approach the police and a case can be registered.

Q: My son got married through internet a few months ago. His wife who stays with us has taken to drinking and smoking. She abuses me and my wife day in and day out. Last week she even assaulted my wife when I complained to her parents, they threatened that they would file a dowry harassment case against us. We are worried.

—Suryakanth Joshi

A: The criminal laws competed with dowry harassment are far severe indeed. If your daughter-in-law lodges the complaint against you, you will have a lot of problems. Please therefore try to built up evidence to show that you have not harassed her for the purpose of dowry. If she lodges a complaint the criminal case is bound to be registered against you. But during the investigation you can convince the police about your innocence. This can happen only if you have some proof about your innocence. A number of innocent parents-in-law have been harassed. It is also true that a number of daughters-in-law are also subjected to untold miseries.

Q: One of my friends persuaded me to join a scheme by which I paid Rs. 5,000/- to become a member and I was expected to get 6 other members and when these 6 members get other members, I get a part of commission. I received some commission for sometime and now I was told apart from getting back my Rs. 5,000/- I will make huge money as commission. During the past 6 months I got back only Rs. 4,000/ - Subsequently I am told company has wound up. Does this not amount to cheating?

—Santhosh Kumar, Bangalore

A: You are a victim of what is known as Ponzi scheme which originated in USA in 1910. A similar scheme is where public are asked to make deposits wherein high returns of interest are promised. One such scheme is Viniv-inc Scheme of Bangalore. In such a scheme, while initial investors get back the money they invest, later investors lose most of the money. There are also other schemes known as Multi Level Marketing Company Schemes. In these schemes, the member is asked to sell products of the company like gold coins, perfumes, household products etc., one such example is Am-Way. Andhra Pradesh Police took up a case against Am-Way, which went up to the Supreme Court. Such schemes come under the purview of Prize Chit and Money Circulation Scheme (Banning) Act 1978. You can lodge a complaint with jurisdictional police about losing money in the Scheme. Most likely you will not get back the money lost.

Q: I gave my house on rent to a decent person in 2000. The agreement was for 3 years. At the end of 3 years, my tenant did not vacate the house. He has sublet the house to some rowdy elements who are into all sorts of illegal activities and they are not vacating the house. How can the police help?

—Nanda Kumar, Mysore

A: The transaction between you and your tenant is purely civil in nature. Police cannot help you to get your house vacated. You have to approach a lawyer for redressal. However, if some illegal activity is taking place in your house, you can alert the local police who can raid the house and book a case against the tenant.

Q: I am a married woman working in an office in Bangalore; I am getting obscene and pornographic email. Sometime I also get obscene messages through SMS. What should I do?

—Rekha (Name changed)

A: Whenever you get such a mail, open the full headers of the mail and you will get to know the IP address from which the mail originated. Through this address police would be able to find out who exactly is harassing you. You may approach the local police for help. They will register a case and investigate.

Q: My son, aged 12 years, is living in a hostel. When he came home for Dasehra holidays, I noticed a change in his behaviour. He had become unusually silent. When I probed the cause, to my dismay, I learnt that he has been subjected to sexual assault by the warden of his hostel. We are from a respectable family and I do not know what to do? I read recently that homosexual Act has been legalized, I am confused.

—(Name withheld on request)

A: Your son is a victim of sodomy which is punishable under Section 377 of the Indian Penal Code. It is a fact that the Delhi High Court recently held that homosexuality between "consenting adults" is not a crime. In this particular case, your son is still a child and the act has been done either without his consent or getting his consent in a forcible manner. You have to lodge a complaint and get the culprit brought to book. If you do not do so, some other child may be subjected to similar attacks and the warden may go scot-free.

Q: Sir, I live in Bangalore. Some goondas and undesirable persons in my locality have put up a small tent stating that they are collecting money and articles for the victims of flood in North Karnataka. They are forcing us to give donation in cash and kind. Is this not an offence?

—Shanta

A: Madam, whenever distress strikes there are any number of unscrupulous people who see opportunity

to make money. Nobody can force you to donate for Flood Relief. If you have been forced to do so, contact the local police. The Police Department has already sent a circular to all the police stations in Karnataka to take action against such people. In case you genuinely want to donate for flood relief, please send your cheque to either the Prime Minister's or Chief Minister's Relief fund. You may also donate through reputed NGOs.

Q: I am a retired government servant. The other day my son was called to Women Police Station, where he was told, a case under dowry harassment is registered against him. My son who is a lawyer asked for a copy of the complaint. When he read the complaint, he found that in the complaint no offence under the Dowry Prohibition Act was brought out. Aren't the police harassing innocent public?

—A. Charles

A: Whenever a complaint about the commission of a cognizable offence is received in a Police Station, Police is expected to draw an FIR. Most of the times, the grouse of the general public is that even when they take genuine cases to the police, the cases do not get registered. In your son's case, the reverse appears to have happened. Merely because the case is registered against your son, it doesn't mean that he will be arrested and sent to jail. Under the Criminal Procedure Code, an investigation has to be conducted by the police who have to ascertain the veracity of the complaint. If your son who is a lawyer has convinced that no offence has taken place, the police will close the case. You need not be unduly perturbed.

Q: While travelling in a KSRTC bus from Mysore to Bangalore, I noticed that my suitcase had been stolen. I alerted the conductor near Bidadi. He was of no

help. Immediately on getting down at Bangalore I gave a complaint to the outpost at the bus stand but they refused to register the case. I do not know what to do. Please help.

—Hemadri, Bangalore

A: The concerned police might not have registered a case since they may be treating your complaint as a complaint of missing suitcase. Technically, they are right, since they are not obliged to register a case regarding missing of any property. If however you had given a complaint that your suitcase was stolen while you were travelling by bus, the police were bound to register a case. Since you were travelling between Mysore and Bangalore, any police station which falls on the way can register and investigate your case. May be you should rephrase your complaint and approach the police again.

As per the Criminal Procedure Code, whenever an information regarding commission of any cognizable offence [Theft, Robbery, Cheating, Murder, Hurt etc., are cognizable offences], the police station concerned must file an FIR, give a copy to the complainant free of cost and investigate the case. If the staffs of the police station refuse to take up the complaint, the complainant can approach either the SP of the district concerned or the Commissioner of Police of the city concerned and lodge a complaint with him. The SP/COP will then direct the concerned police to register the case and take up investigation.

The Police Head quarter has recently sent a circular to all SP's and COP's that registration of criminal case shall be done in a free manner and if any complainant approaches SP/COP with the complaint of a cognizable case, the same should be got registered.

Q: My daughter was admitted to a nursing home with severe pain in the abdomen. She was having high

temperature. The doctors at the nursing home did not treat her properly and her condition worsened. Within 24 hours of admission she died. She was only 25 years old. Can I take up a case against the Doctors of the Nursing Home?

–K.H. Venkatesh Gowda

A: Any death caused due to a negligent act can be reason for a registration of a cognizable case. In your case how can you prove that the doctors in the nursing home were negligent in their duties? If there is evidence that by a negligent act the death was caused, the case can be taken up. Many people die in hospital due to various reasons every day. If cases are registered against doctors for each death, there may be no doctors available to treat patients. It is also a fact that many negligent doctors, quacks etc., have been successfully prosecuted. The fact in each situation should disclose a cognizable offence for a case to be taken up.

Q: My daughter aged 22 years fell in love with a boy belonging to a different community. We were opposed to this affair. In the interest of my daughter's future, we got her married to the same boy. Since, she was our only daughter, we gave a lot of ornaments to her and also gave costly presents to our son-in-law. Within 10 months of marriage, my daughter's husband and in-laws started harassing her. She committed suicide recently. Can we take up a case against our son-in-law?

A: In this case, there appears to be no demand for dowry by your son-in-law or any body. But if the husband or any relative of the husband subjects a woman to cruelty [cruelty means conduct of a nature which is likely to drive a woman to commit suicide] such a person can be hauled up under Section 498A of the IPC wherein he can be punished with imprisonment for a term extending up to 3 years. You may lodge a

complaint against your son-in-law.

Q: I am embarrassed to ask this question, but I am forced to seek your advice. I am married since 15 years and we have a son and a daughter. My wife is very ambitious and wants to lead a very lavish life which I cannot afford. Of late I have noticed that she has developed friendship with a person who is a college student and she is having a sexual affair with him. Can anything be done about it?

—Name withheld on request

A: If any person has sexual intercourse with the wife of another man, without the consent of another man, then he can be punished for an offence under adultery. However, for a case to be registered by the police for an offence of adultery, the affected person [in this case you] needs to lodge a complaint in the police station. Please note that your wife will not be liable for any punishment. Considering the above you may take appropriate action.

Q: I read an advertisement in a leading newspaper offering some goods at a fabulous discount. I had asked to send Rs. 1,000/- by Money Order which I did. After one week I received a parcel, wherein I found that the article sent to me was defective and was not even worth Rs. 100/-. Can I give complaint of cheating?

—Mr. Prakash Badiga

A: Instead of approaching the police station, you should approach the Consumer Forum wherein you may get some compensation. If you approach the police, a criminal case will be registered against the concerned. But he is not bound to make goods loss incurred by you.

Q: I took a loan of Rs. 35 lakhs from a person for taking up construction of an apartment block. I promised to

give the lender 2 flats for the amount lent. He however insisted that I should give him 7 cheques for Rs. 5 lakh each as a security. I gave him the cheques without writing the date or name of the payee on the cheque, but I mentioned the amount and affixed my signature. Due to some litigation, I was not able to get the site and take up building work. In the meanwhile the lender kept on forcing me to return the amount saying he does not want to have a flat. Since I had no money I could not return the amount. He later filed a complaint against me for cheque bounce and a case is registered against me. I need your help.

–Ramaswamy, Bangalore

A: There is nothing wrong if the lender insisted on some sort of security like a post dated cheque while he lent you Rs. 35 lakhs. You should not have given him cheque leaves without putting the name of the Payee or the date. Obviously the lender has inserted the date and name, presented the cheques in the bank wherein they bounced. A criminal offence has been made out against you and the FIR taken up against you is in order. You will have to face prosecution. Please engage a good lawyer to defend you.

Q: I have a two-wheeler and ride to work. Last week at about 9 pm near Marathalli one traffic constable stopped me and asked me to show the documents. I had xerox copy of my Driving License. He said that this is not in order and demanded Rs.1,000/- as bribe, finally he settled for Rs.200/-. Is it not robbery on the part of traffic police?

–Venkatesha Murthy

A: A traffic constable is not authorized to check documents of motor vehicles. Normally officers not below the rank of ASI in Bangalore City and SIs elsewhere are only authorized to check vehicles and impose fine. The top police officials of Bangalore City

have given instructions that traffic police should not routinely check vehicle riders to see if they are in possession of valid documents. Document check is done only when a vehicle is flagged for some traffic violation. Hence the constable who stopped you and demanded bribe has certainly exceeded his limits. If you have noted down his name, please inform Additional Commissioner of Police-Traffic, Bangalore City who will take necessary action. Henceforth do not pay bribes to any traffic policeman.

Q: My neighbour is having a ferocious dog. The other day, this dog attacked me and bit me. I had to take medication. Can I file a case against my neighbour?

—Upadhyaya. S.L

A: The incident in question does not come under the purview of criminal law and falls within the civil law. Please consult an advocate for redressal of your complaint.

Q: My son received an e-mail from General Electric Company stating that he has been selected for a job in England and that he should send Rs. 50,000/- for getting travel documents like visa and also to pay advance for a house in London. After my son paid the first instalment, he was asked to pay Rs. 25,000/- more for customs and other formalities. He paid this amount too. He was also asked to send bank details, passport details etc., which he did. But the appointment order never came. What to do?

—Usha Sharma

A: No reputed firm approaches individuals with job offers through e-mail. You must realize that recruitment does not take place in this manner and no recruiter will ask for any money for giving a job. Your son should not have paid the requisite amount. He has been a victim of cheating. Please lodge a police complaint. Since the perpetrator is sitting abroad, it

is very difficult to get him to India and face trial. Your money is lost. Please be more careful in future before parting with your hard earned money.

Q: My son, before going abroad 2 years ago, sold his car to a person in Mysore and filled up all the relevant forms. He also took acknowledgement of sale from the purchaser. He informed the concerned RTO in writing about selling the car. When I went to RTO's office last week I enquired about the transfer of my son's car. I was taken aback to know that till date the car has not been transferred to the name of the purchaser. I am worried. What course of action should I take?

—Lakshmi Narayana

A: Some unscrupulous persons deliberately do not get vehicles purchased by them registered in their names. In your son's case the same has happened. Please approach the Transport Commissioner, Bangalore with all the details and he will take necessary action. If you have copies of Form No-29 and the sale letter, you need not worry and your son will not face any trouble if the vehicle meets with an accident or violates some traffic rules.

Q: I paid for the recharge of my cell phone through my credit card. Instead of debiting Rs. 300/-, Rs. 3,300/- was debited. I immediately called up the cell phone company and informed the mistake. They stated that they will credit back the excess amount to my card within 4 working days. Even though 15 days are over the amount is not credited to my bank. I am a senior citizen. I want to file a criminal case. Please help.

—M. Sukumar

A: Many a time such incidents happen when you make payment for services or purchases electronically. Normally the excess amount is credited back to your card. This is called reverse credit. Please check up

from your card issuing bank whether the amount has been credited or not. This incident does not come under the purview of criminal law.

Q: A week ago, I was driving my car in Bangalore along with my husband at night. When I made a right turn near a traffic signal, one motorcyclist came at break neck speed and seeing my car applied brakes suddenly. Due to this, he skidded and fell down. We immediately came out of our car and with the help of onlookers took the motorcyclist in my car to a near by hospital and got him admitted. The next day I enquired about the welfare of the injured person and was told he had sustained a fracture. Yesterday, two policemen came to my house and summoned me to the police station. At the police station, the Inspector told me that a case has been filed against me by the injured motorcyclist and that I need to be arrested and my vehicle seized for RTO inspection. I explained the incident but he did not believe me. I became a victim for doing a good Samaritan act. What should I do?

—Suvarna M. Bangalore

A: You are not the first person to get involved in a criminal case for doing a good deed. A number of motorists commit a big mistake of not informing the police whenever their vehicle is involved in an accident. In the instant case, the injured motorcyclist has made a false allegation against you so that he can get a sizeable amount as compensation for the hospital treatment he undergoes. Immediately after admitting the injured to the hospital, you should have informed the concerned police about the accident. For having not done so, the needle of suspicion is pointing towards you. Many traffic junctions in Bangalore have surveillance cameras and you can request the police to see the video footage, to prove that you are innocent. However, if there was no camera near the place of incident, it is very difficult to convince the cops that

you are innocent. Since a case of causing grievous injury by rash and negligent driving might have been taken up against you, you are bound to be arrested and released on bail. Your car needs to be inspected by the RTO. During the inspection, you can prove that it was not involved in any accident. It is most likely that the police will file a chargesheet in this case, since they may have no evidence to disprove the version of injured motorcyclist. You should engage a good lawyer and fight the case in the court. It may take years it you contest the case. I really feel sorry for you. At least henceforth inform the police, when you see any accident or get involved in any accident.

Q: I see a large number of two-wheeler riders in both Hubli and Belgaum riding without helmets. Is the helmet rule not applicable in North Karnataka?

—Jayatheertha Joshi, Hubli

A: The rule applies to the entire state of Karnataka. It is likely that the officers in those areas are not enforcing the rule. I may also mention here that wearing a helmet protects the life of a two-wheeler rider. Rule or no rule, wearing a helmet is advisable for both riders and pillion riders of two-wheelers.

Q: I see a number of two-wheeler riders in Bangalore not wearing helmets with ISI markings. Why are the Traffic Police keeping quiet?

—Sunil Sharma, Bangalore

A: The Bangalore Traffic Police is heavily overworked and regulation of traffic itself takes much of its resources. It is impossible and impractical for policemen on the road to stop each and every two-wheeler rider and check whether he is wearing an ISI marked helmet or otherwise. It is assumed that the rider protects his head by wearing a proper helmet. A senior police officer's son died sometime ago, by not

properly fixing the helmet straps. More than enforcement, there must be a voluntary action for safety.

Q: A business partner who lives in Jalandhar owed me 10 lakh rupees. I got a case registered against him, but he is not appearing in the Court. The Bangalore Court has issued a warrant of arrest in his name, but the Bangalore police is not taking any action to execute the warrant and arrest the person. What is the remedy?

—Chandra Shekar Iyer, Bangalore

A: It is always difficult for policemen from one state to go to another state and arrest persons from there. Many a time the police team may not have proper descriptive particulars, address etc., of the person to be arrested. It would have been prudent if you had got a warrant issued for execution by Jalandhar police. Normally, CID is a nodal agency for getting warrants from across the state executed. You may also seek the help of Punjab CID.

Q: My neighbour has rented the first floor of his house to a Recreation Club. Every day from morning to mid night hundreds of people visit this club and they park their vehicles in a haphazard manner on the footpath. It is difficult for me to even take out my car. I am fed up. Can't the police do something?

—Sadashiva Gowda, Mysore

A: Please approach the traffic police of your area and explain your problem. They may call the office bearers of the club and advise them about parking of vehicles by the club members.

Q: On 25th July when I was travelling in a BMTC bus, my mobile phone was stolen. The next day I went to Ulsoor Police Station and lodged a complaint of theft.

The ASI there told me that he will accept the complaint only if I write that the phone is lost and not show it as stolen. I had no other go but to comply. I want to ask whether the Police Manual authorizes police stations to change the contents of complaint. Will this not dilute the gravity of the offence? I suspect that there is a nexus between the police, pick pocket and receivers and that is why such a thing is happening.

—P. Kaledasa Reddy, Bangalore

A: Technically the act of picking one's pocket will amount to an offence of theft. In cases where a person finds himself to be relieved of a valuable on his person, it is very difficult to ascertain whether the loss is due to theft or otherwise. Many a time jewellery, watches, cell phones etc., fall away without the knowledge of the owner. Hence it is very difficult to say whether missing of a valuable item is due to theft or otherwise. As per the Criminal Procedure Code, whenever a complaint of theft is lodged in Police Station, the SHO is bound to register an offence and take up investigation. After registering a case, the police officer is competent to close the case if (a) the value of the property is very meager (b) if the property stolen cannot be easily identified (eg: a bag of apples) etc. If any police officer refuses to register a case concerning a cognizable offence, the complainant can approach a superior police officer, in this case the Commissioner of Police, Bangalore. I do not agree with your contention that police have nexus with pick pocket and receivers and therefore do not register cases. Normally, policemen at the stations do not want to get the cases registered in order to show that the crime rate in their area has not gone up. Also investigation is a time consuming process.

Q: I am a law abiding citizen. So many times traffic police have affixed stickers on my car stating that I have parked in a no parking area. I have never parked in

an area having No Parking sign boards. Don't you think that the traffic police are harassing me?

—B.K. Sinha

A: In such cases you should immediately contact the concerned traffic police station and ascertain why they have given you a notice when you have not parked in a No Parking area. It is not possible for police to put no parking sign boards every 100 meters. By convention, on roads which are one-way, parking is allowed only on one side of the road. This is understood by the road users even if there is no sign board.

Q: I am a frequent traveller from Bangalore to Cochin. Whenever I reach Cantonment Station in the night and come out to hail an auto rickshaw, a bunch of auto drivers approaches me asking to board their vehicles. When I sit in the auto they demand extra money above the actual meter reading. When I approach the traffic constable at the spot to intervene, he advises me to take a pre paid auto. Why are the police not tackling the auto mafia?

—Rajesh Vatsala

A: If every person who wants an auto at the Railway Station gets into a queue, gets the pre paid auto token, no auto driver will behave the way he does. Some commuters want to reach their destination quickly, and hence come out of the station and hail empty autos on the road. Such persons are fleeced. Some traffic cops at the railway stations are not actual traffic policemen, they belong to railway police. When any auto driver demands excess fare from you, note down the number and send a complaint to the Additional Commissioner of Police, Traffic.

Q: At the traffic signals in Bangalore there are a lot of transgender who harass people. We also find a number

of women carrying small children begging for money, some children do gymnastics and use the footpath to show their skills. Can't the traffic police do something about them?

—V. Mahesh

A: It is necessary that police and the civic authorities join together to round up beggars not only at a traffic junctions but elsewhere in the city and put them in beggar's home. A sustained effort is necessary to clear the traffic junctions of beggars.

Q: My daughter is studying in 10th standard. Recently she started getting phone calls asking for sexual favours. When she shouted at one of the callers, he asked her as to why she has advertised her services on the internet. We learnt that some person has uploaded a nude and morphed photo of my daughter and stated that she is available for sexual favour. We are shattered, please help.

—Name withheld on request

A: Your daughter is a victim of Cyber Crime. It is most likely that persons known to her have committed this act. This act is punishable under IT Act-2000. Please lodge a complaint in the Cyber Police Station which is situated in CID Headquarters, Palace Road, Bangalore.

Q: The rule of no smoking in public places is not followed properly. Police are also not enforcing this rule. One day I saw two traffic policemen happily smoking at a public place. Doesn't the rule apply to them?

—Karthik V. Rao, X Standard Student, Bangalore

A: No smoking rule in public place applies to everyone including policemen. Unfortunately, there are not enough persons to enforce this rule. Due to lack of enforcement, many are flouting the rule. As a student you should have pointed out to the policemen about

their action. They would have been ashamed (Policemen would be sensitized about this matter).

Q: I signed surety to one of my colleague who borrowed Rs. 2 lakhs from the Employees Co-operative Credit Society of my factory. My colleague left for Australia and his services were terminated. Since I have signed surety for the loan, the society is recovering loan instalment from my salary. My efforts to contact my colleague in Australia have become futile. I spoke to his relatives in Bangalore, but they have expressed their inability in the matter. How can I recover this money?

—R. Shanmugam, Bangalore

A: The matter which you disclose does not come under the purview of criminal law, since your colleague has not committed any criminal act. You may approach your factory employers and find out whether any outstanding payment was due to your colleague which could be set off against the loan taken. You may file a civil case through a lawyer to recover your money.

Q: My neighbour who is a politician demolished a portion of the compound wall built by me and constructed a separate wall forcibly encroaching on my land. I went to the police station and lodged a complaint but they did not do any thing. I approached the court, the case is still pending. Will not the action of the politician amount to contempt of Court?

—Name withheld on request

A: If your neighbour had trespassed into your land, a criminal case was made out. I do not understand why the police did not register the case based on your complaint. Now that you have approached the court, allow the law to take its course. Your neighbour's action does not amount to contempt.

Q: Many of our footpaths near the busy market places are encroached upon by hawkers and police are

turning a blind eye. What is the problem in clearing the hawkers?

—P.V. Krishna Kumar

A: Hawkers on footpaths are a problem not only in Bangalore city, but also in highly developed countries too. It is not possible for the limited traffic policemen to clear the footpaths on a day-to-day basis. Unless separate hawking zones are created and unless public resolve not to buy from road side vendors this problem will continue.

Q: When my wife and I were working in London, our daughter was born and she became a citizen of UK. When she was 5 years old we relocated to India. She still has British passport. Is it necessary to register her as a foreigner with the Bangalore Police?

—Kuldeep Sharma

A: Since your daughter is a British citizen by birth and continues to have British passport, she is technically a foreigner and requires to be registered in the Foreigner's Registration office, Bangalore. She can renounce British citizenship or she can also be holding dual citizenship. Please visit web site of Ministry of Home Affairs, Govt. of India at www.mha.nic.in for more details.

Q: I have a licence to posses a non-prohibited bore revolver and I am required to purchase a weapon and produce it for inspection to police within the next 4 months. Most of the imported second hand weapons are very expensive and unaffordable. What should I do?

—L.N. Mukherjee

A: The Indian Ordnance Factory produces good quality small weapons which are not very expensive. Since your requirement of weapon is only for self protection, you may buy a new Indian made weapon.

Q: I want to apply for my passport, I am told that police verification for the same will take a very long time

and that it is better to go in for Tatkal Passport.

—Shylaja, Gulbarga

A: Whenever you apply for an Indian Passport, local police have to verify whether you are living at the address given by you and whether you are involved or wanted in any criminal case. If you have changed your residence in the past two three years, the process of verification will take a longer time, since your antecedents have to be verified at the previous address also. Applications for Tatkal Passport are made only if there is a great urgency. After you apply for Passport, police officers of your area go to your house for verification. The process does not take too long.

Q: My 18-year-old daughter is having an affair since one year with a boy, younger to her and belonging to another religion. The boy and his parents have brainwashed my daughter to give up our religion and convert to their religion. Because of this, my daughter is rebelling with our family. We are very much disturbed.

—Name withheld

A: If any girl under 18 years of age is enticed from her lawful guardians without the consent of such guardians, an offence of kidnapping is made out. If the kidnapping is with an intention for the purpose of prostitution or marriage, serious punishment is contemplated. Since your daughter is above 18 years of age, even if she is enticed by her boyfriend or parents, no offence is made out. This is a very delicate problem and needs to be handled sensitively. It is better both the families meet and thrash things out.

Q: My daughter is 24 years old; fell in love with a Class-IV employee working in her office. She ran away from home a month back. We recently received a call from Tirupathi that she and her friend got married in a

temple. She lived with her friend for 5 days and they both had physical relationship. We have forcibly brought her back home. Can a case be taken up against the boy?

—Name withheld

A: Since your daughter is an adult and went to Tirupathi on her own accord, her boyfriend cannot be charged for any offence. Since the marriage appears to be not legal, the physical relation the boy had with your daughter amounts to an offence of rape. He can be prosecuted. You have to take a call on this.

Q: Lot of construction activities are going on for improving infrastructure of Bangalore. Because of this roads have become narrow. On the narrow roads buses stop holding up traffic further, such as, Chord Road, Rajajinagar. Why can't the traffic police do something about this?

—H.V. Gurumurthy

A: Traffic management is not the only concern of the police. Other civil agencies like Municipalities, Public Works Department, Transport Department etc., need to be actively involved in traffic management. Wherever there is a co-ordination between all the agencies, problems are less. In the instant case since buses have to stop at some place and that the road is narrow one has to bear with the problem.

Q: I am a senior citizen living with my wife in our ancestor's home. My children are abroad. Now-a-days criminal are attacking couples like us. Could you suggest some safety measures?

—B. Shivalinge Gowda, Mysore

A: As families become nuclear, safety issues become a concern. Please install security devices to your residence. For example for the front door you can install a camera with phone facility, wherein you can

talk to the stranger without opening the door. You can make your front and back doors stronger. Don't follow the same routine while going out of the house. Don't open doors to strangers. Don't keep heavy cash or costly articles at home. If you employ a servant, get his antecedents checked by the police. Be wary of strangers. When you leave home for long durations keep your neighbours informed. Please keep a dog at home; they are not only good companions but also good guards.

Q: I went to Japan recently with my wife. Before going abroad, my wife had to attend a wedding and she had brought her gold ornaments from Bank locker and had kept them at home. When we were in Japan, our neighbours informed that somebody had broken into our house. We cut short our tour and returned home to see that our almirah had been ransacked and jewellery valued at more than ₹ 10 lakhs stolen. Even though 4 months are over police are clueless. Are the police not interested in detecting this case?

–Ramamurthy, Beluru

A: It was unwise on your part to keep high value items at your home, when you were going out for long periods of time. Normally only 40 out of 100 such offences get detected. Since the jurisdictional police do not have any clues in this matter, they may close this case as undetected. You should have gone in for insurance.

Q: My friend bought an industrial shed. When he went to occupy the same, he found a security guard who had been employed by the former owner of the shed. My friend asked the guard to go away, but the guard refused, stating that he will leave the place only if his unpaid wages amounting to Rupees forty thousand are paid by my friend. What should he do?

–Narayana Chalapathi

A: The act of the security guard amounts to criminal trespass. Ask your friend to lodge an FIR in the jurisdictional police station. Your friend is not obliged to pay wages to the guard.

Q: I have applied for a housing loan with one of the companies which had advertised on the internet. Please advise me whether I should go ahead or not.

—Ramachandra B.R.

A: It is always advisable that while doing financial transactions through the internet one must be very careful. Why don't you approach any Bank or reputed financial institutions for a home loan?

Q: This refers to your answer for my question last week. Perhaps I did not present my question properly. I have a problem with my neighbour regarding our boundary and 1½ years ago I filed a case against him in the Court. The case is still pending. My neighbour has constructed a compound at my site 4 months back. Does this not amount to contempt?

—Name withheld on request

A: When a case is pending before the Court, it is advisable to maintain the status quo. Your neighbour has not done that; please bring this fact to the notice of the Court which will take appropriate action.

Q: My colleagues want to form a group in Bangalore to make presentations on road safety in all educational institutions. How to go about it?

—Dr. M.M. Bagali

A: Kindly approach the Additional Commissioner of Police Traffic, Bangalore City.

Q: The other day I saw strangers vandalise vehicles parked on our street. A policeman was coming that way. When I told the policeman about the vandals the

policeman said that his duty hours are over and went away even when the vandals were within his sight. Is it not the duty of the police to prevent crime?

—Vasudevan

A: A police officer is expected to be on duty 24 hours a day. Even while he is on leave or on tour he is expected to perform his duty. I am surprised that you did not get any help from the policeman who came your way. There are black sheep within the department. It is duty of the police to prevent and detect crime. You should have dialled 100 and sought help.

Q: Some person is sending offensive SMSes to me through my cell phone. What action can be taken against the sender?

—Uma Joshi, Belgaum

A: As per the amended IT Act, which has come into force only recently, if any person sends offensive messages which cause annoyance through communication devices, he can be imprisoned for a term which may extend up to 3 years. You may therefore contact jurisdictional police to lodge a complaint.

Q: I have observed that police officers do their duty meticulously whenever there are VIP visits or whenever there are security threats. After 15 days of high alertness they become lax. They stop putting barricades, they stop mounting guards, they stop checking people and vehicles etc. Why is this so?

—Kusuma M.

A: Whenever any security threat is perceived, it is natural for any security agency to concentrate and neutralize the threat. While police remain alert all the time, they may not be deploying most of their resources on targeted places all the time. When a perceived threat passes off, the extra resources that are deployed to checkmate the threat are slowly withdrawn. The

limited manpower at the command of the police needs to be deployed effectively.

Q: I commute from home to college in buses. I observe that seats reserved for women and elderly are invariably occupied by others. Can't the police take action?

—Venkateshachary, Mangalore

A: Whenever complaints are received, action is definitely taken against the concerned. It is the duty of the bus conductor to enforce the reservation rule. However, mere enforcement of the rule does not solve the problem. We have to develop a strong civic sense. What prevents you and other commuters from telling the culprit that what he is doing is wrong? If he is shamed, he may not commit the mistake again.

Q: In your reply for a question last week you have stated that a rape case could be booked against the husband of a girl who got married in a temple, if the parents of the girls have complained. When the girl had physical contact willingly, how can this amount to rape?

—Lakshmi Narayana Kumble

A: The Indian Penal Code states that rape is committed when a person has sexual intercourse with a woman even with her consent when the man knows that he is not her husband and that consent was given because the woman believes herself to be lawfully married to him. If two adults exchange garlands in a temple and state that they are married, this marriage does not amount to a legal wedding. Therefore on the complaint of the girl's parent a case of rape could be registered against the boy.

Q: There is no lane discipline on highways even when there are 4-lane roads. Many slow moving vehicles use the right side of the road; actually they should use

the left side of the road. Because of this overtaking happens from the left resulting in accidents. Can't the traffic police take action on drivers of slow moving vehicles using the right side of the road?

—Vivek

A: Many accidents on highways occur because fast moving vehicles overtake from the left, and while so overtaking, dash against vehicles parked on the left side of the road. Unless road users are properly educated periodically and unless licenses of errant drivers are suspended, such accidents will continue to happen.

Q: What in your opinion is the root cause of traffic indiscipline in Bangalore?

—Gayathri

A: I feel that for most of the traffic violators in Bangalore, existing fines are not deterrent. Since the fines are quite low most of the violators are prepared to pay the fine and violate the rule. The fines should be exemplary. We should also think of imposing prison terms for repeated violators.

Q: My housekeeper's son was murdered last year. He approached the Investigating Officer for a copy of the post mortem report. He was told that copy can be given only if some bribe is paid. Should we pay money for post mortem report? Also the Investigating Officer has mentioned names of some witnesses who were not near the scene of offence. Is this not wrong?

—M.V. Nahusha Raj

A: No money need to be paid for getting a copy of the post mortem report. Please lodge a complaint against the Investigating Officer for demanding bribe. Please also bring to the notice of higher authorities about mentioning the names of people who are not at all connected with this case. Normally cases of murder

are being supervised by Senior Officers. Please approach the SP/DCP concerned.

Q: My daughter aged 13 years is a sports person. She has been put in a sports training camp. She complains that her coach is not behaving properly with her and he indulges in unwelcome petting. Can anything be done about it?

—R. Rameshan

A: Many children get molested at the hands of elders and many a time they are not even aware of being abused. I suggest you to go to the coaching class and observe the activities of the coach. After assessing the situation you may lodge a complaint in the jurisdictional police station for an offence of molestation which is a serious crime. You may also consider lodging a complaint before the Child Welfare Committee in Bangalore. Before taking any action please make sure that the act of the coach is not an innocent act.

Q: My husband is not happy with me ever since we got married. We are a working couple and for silly reasons he harasses me. Ever since marriage we have not had any sexual relationship. Can any action be taken against my husband?

—Name withheld on request

A: An interpretation of Section 498(a) of Indian Penal Code would reveal that, denial of the conjugal rights to a wife by the husband (which may cause grave injury to the mental or physical health of the woman) as cruelty. Denial of conjugal rights can also be a valid reason for seeking divorce. If you are inclined, you may get a case registered against your husband.

Q: My unmarried daughter works in a BPO and she has to work during nights. One of her supervisors is constantly demanding sexual favours from her and is

threatening that he will get her terminated from work if she does not comply. My daughter has become a mental wreck. Please advice.

—**Deshpande R.S.**

A: The action of your daughter's supervisor amounts to an offence under Section 509 of the Indian Penal Code. In the famous Vishaka judgment, the Supreme Court addressed the problem of sexual harassment at work place. Consequent to this judgment, the Government came out with a bill called Protection of Women against Sexual Harassment at work place. It is now the duty of the employer to provide a safe working environment to the women employees in his organization and that it also becomes his duty to enquire into all complaints by aggrieved women. Let your daughter complain against the supervisor to her employer.

Q: Recently I got an e-mail from a woman living in an African country proposing marriage. She stated that she wants to leave her country and come to India and if I agree to have a formal marriage she will give me 10 percent of her inheritance which she will get only if she gets married. She said that after two months we can take a divorce. I did not reply. She has sent me one more mail. Is this some kind of a fraud?

—**Sudheer Kumar, Bangalore**

A: The mail you received is a new type of fraud being perpetrated by Nigerian fraudsters. Once you agree for the proposal you would be pestered for sending some money so that you can get 10 percent of the inheritance. Please don't fall a prey to such tricks.

Q: My daughter aged 25 years came into contact with an Indian who is settled abroad. This person after having friendship with my daughter over internet for about 6 months proposed marriage to her. He has sent his photos and other details. My daughter appears to be happy with him. He is willing to come to India and

get married. He is asking my daughter to get her passport ready. Should we go ahead with this proposal?

—Sathish Kulkarni

A: Many proposals for marriage over the internet turn out to be frauds. I have come across a case wherein a girl from Karnataka got married to a boy in USA and when she landed at her husband's place she learnt that her husband had already got married. She was made to work as a maid in their house and with a great difficulty she returned to India. Please therefore check the antecedents of the boy who has proposed. Unless you are very certain about the character of the boy don't agree for the wedding.

Q: I'm a 21-year-old Muslim male. I fell in love with a 17 years old Muslim girl, who was a native of Kashmir studying in Bangalore, and got married (nikah) to her with her consent. After marriage her mother came down from Kashmir and got me arrested on charges of kidnapping, rape and child marriage. I agree I have made a mistake but never intended to commit a crime. I will be very thankful if you would advice me on this.

—Tabrez (name changed)

A: Since you have taken away a girl below 18 years of age out of the keeping of her lawful guardian, you have committed an offence of kidnapping. Since the marriage between both of you is not lawful you have also committed an offence of rape. You will have to face the consequences of your action. Please engage a good lawyer to defend you in the court of law.

Q: As representative of our Apartment Association, I had made complaints to the city traffic authorities regarding the increased vehicular traffic in our locality. The copy of the complaint was endorsed to DG&IGP. A copy of a complaint was also sent to City Police

Commissioner. But no action seems to have been taken so far.

—P.S.S. Nair

A: Please approach the Deputy Commissioner of Police, Traffic (West) with your complaint. He will definitely take action.

Q: I live in the last house in a narrow cul-de-sac. My neighbour parks his car in the lane, obstructing 4-wheeler entry into my premises. I complained to police and suggested they make the lane a NO PARKING zone, but police merely issued letters cautioning them against random parking which might inconvenience others. Despite this, my neighbour persists in parking his car causing obstruction to me. What is the remedy?

—S. Govindaraj

A: Request the DCP (Traffic) to declare a part of the road as 'No Parking' area. After this happens if your neighbour parks in a no parking zone you may request the traffic police to tow away his vehicle. He will have to pay a stiff penalty for towing charges. If his vehicle is towed away three, four times he will learn a lesson.

Q: My neighbour who is working for the Karnataka Government, is having a 10-year-old girl as a domestic help in his house. Is this not against law?

—Sudha Narasimha

A: The action of your neighbour in engaging a child as household help is illegal. Even as per the Karnataka Government Civil Service Rules, no Government servant shall keep a child below 14 years in his/her house as domestic help. Please write a letter to the Head of the Department where your neighbour is working. You may also alert the Child Welfare Committee of your area.

Q: My house was burgled about 4 months ago and property worth Rupees one lakh was stolen. A case has been registered in the Police Station. So far I have no idea of what has happened to the case.

—K. Shankaran

A: Detection of theft cases normally take a long time. However, if a case does not get detected within 3 to 4 months the Investigating Officer will file a report to the Court stating that the case is undetected. At a later date if the case is detected, it is reopened, the culprit is nabbed, property recovered and case charge sheeted. It appears that your case is not yet detected.

Q: I filed a complaint in a Police Station stating that my neighbour has given a threat to my life and that he also abused me in vulgar language and once slapped me. Now I received a notice stating that my case is closed. Why is the case closed?

—C. Chandra Shekar

A: It is likely that the Investigating Officer has not found any truth in the accusation made by you. During the investigation if it comes to light that a case is filed by a wrong interpretation of law or on a wrong narration of fact, the case can be closed. However before closing, the complainant has to be given an opportunity to contest the claim of the Investigating Officer. After hearing the complainant the magistrate decides whether the case can be closed or otherwise. Since you have now an opportunity to comment on the findings of the IO, if you feel, you can contest the same.

Q: I am a 25-year-old woman. I had a love marriage with a person who was a teacher. His parents did not know about this marriage. I have 2 children. Now my husband has joined Police Department as a SI. He is planning to marry another girl and his parents are

fully supporting. What should I do?

—Name withheld

A: You can approach senior police officers and request them to stop your husband from marrying a second time. I don't know whether your marriage is legally valid or otherwise. You may approach an advocate. Incidentally, a person named Dharam who was working in Delhi Municipal Corporation had promised marriage to a colleague of his, had sexual affair with her, had obtained eight thousand rupees from her for his higher education and later abandoned her. In this case the Delhi Court had held that Dharam's action amounts to cheating.

Q: My father was working in the Police Department as a Head Constable. In the year 1995 he was sent on duty out of State. He never returned and he is missing since then. Can I get a job in the police department on compassionate ground?

—Mohan Kumar, Nelamangala

A: When your father went missing, a missing case would have been filed in a police station. Since he is not traced the case would have been closed. As your father is not traced for more than 7 years it can be presumed that he is dead. On the basis of his death while on duty, you can apply for a government job.

Q: I run a small eating joint. Recently some officials of Labour Department with the help of police officers conducted a raid on my premises, detected that I was employing child labour and have filed a case against me. When senior IAS/IPS officers are keeping young children as domestic help, is it fair on the part of the department to book a case against me?

—R. Shanbhag, Hubli

A: Under the Child Labour Prohibition and Regulation Act, employing children below 14 years of age in tea-stalls, hotels and domestic households is prohibited.

Q: I am working as a teacher in a private school. I got married 3 months ago. My husband and his family members are constantly insulting me that I did not bring from my parents any valuables. I did not care for this. Recently my husband dropped me in my parent's house. He and his family are telling that they will take me back home only if I resign from my job. What should I do?

—S. Suma

A: The action of your husband and his family members amount to an offence of dowry harassment. You may lodge a complaint with jurisdictional police. Please do not resign from the job you are holding.

Q: I had engaged an advocate to represent me in a civil case. He took a fee of Rs 5000 from me but is not attending court when my case comes and refuses to return my money. Can I lodge a complaint against him for cheating with the police?

—K. Paramesh

A: For any act to be considered as criminal there must be a criminal mind or mens rea. The act of your counsel may not attract criminal law. Please complain against him with the Bar Council of India.

Q: I am an unemployed graduate. A few weeks ago, at about 11 pm, I was sitting on a scooter parked on a road and was waiting for my friend. Two constables came there and asked me what I was doing there at that time. They were not satisfied with my reply, took me to the Station and alleged that was I trying to steal the scooter. They kept me in the Station the entire night, beat me black and blue and released me the next morning, after warning me that if I told anyone about the incident, I would be jailed. Can you take action against them?

—Virupaksha

A: Please approach the State Human Rights Commission apart from the DG & IGP, Karnataka State and narrate your experience. Certainly action against the guilty cops would be taken. You should have gone to a Government Hospital immediately on release from the Police Station and should have stated the facts and taken first aid. It could have made your case very strong.

Q: Last week someone used my e-mail ID and sent mails to my friends stating that I am in London attending a conference and that I have lost my wallet, passport etc. The culprit asked my friends to send money through Western Union Money Transfer. One friend sent Rs 5000/-. I came to know about this after I received calls asking whether I am back in Bangalore. What should I do?

—Vasant Ramarao Kulkarni

A: Obviously someone has hacked into your e-mail account. You might have unwittingly disclosed your login ID and password to a phishing mail which has resulted in such an action. Please lodge a complaint in the Police Station. Change your password at once.

Q: I am in love with a girl who belongs to a community different than mine. We want to get married, but her parents are dead against this. My friend is suggesting that we should run away from our homes and get married. I am not in favour of this and want approval of all concerned for the marriage. My friend is now saying that if I don't agree to her suggestion, she will commit suicide and name me as the person responsible in her suicide note. I am perturbed. If something happens to her will I be arrested?

—Arun

A: Abetment of suicide amounts to an offence under section 306 of the IPC. However, the facts and

circumstances explained by you do not attract this provision of law if your friend commits suicide. Why don't you and some elders of your family approach the girl's parents and explain the situation?

Q: I represent the security wing of a multi-national company. We employ a large number of contract workers. Since we are highly security conscious, we wanted police verification of each contract employee. The fees prescribed by the Bangalore police is exorbitant and hence we are unable to get proper verification done. Can you suggest a remedy?

—Capt. Mani

A: Compared to the fee charged by private agencies, the fee prescribed by the Government is not high. What I would advise is that you get each employee's personal data and photo and send the same to the SP of the District from where the employee hails for verification. There may be some delay in response but it is worth waiting. If a contract employee is being employed for a very short term, you may not assign him any sensitive work.

Q: I come from a respectable family and have a good standing in society. Some persons who are inimical to me got me falsely implicated in a non-bailable case. The police arrested me and sent me to judicial custody. I had to spend four days in jail. After investigation, the police have closed the case as mistake of fact. Because of my arrest, I have suffered humiliation. Can I take up a case against the police?

—Name withheld

A: Under Sec 182 of the IPC, whoever gives false information to a public servant with intent to cause that public servant to use his lawful power to the injury of another person can be punished for imprisonment for a term which may extend to six months. You can file a complaint against your enemies

for this offence. However since this is a non-cognizable offence, you have to approach a court for registration of your complaint.

Q: I am a resident of CIL Layout, Hebbal. Every day from 8.45 - 9.45 in the morning 25 to 30 labourers sit opposite my house, park their vehicles haphazardly on the road and create problems. I have complained to local police station as well as to Hoysala. So far there is no relief. Please take action.

—Karthik

A: Please write to the Commissioner of Police, Bangalore City and mark a copy to the Additional Commissioner of Police, Traffic, Bangalore. They would take necessary action. Blocking a way amounts to an offence.

Q: During Vaikunta Ekadashi day at Yalahanka Venkateshwara Temple, one police constable abused me in filthy language, held my neck and said that he will fix me in a criminal case. This happened because I asked him to do his duty to regulate the crowd. Whom should I complain to?

—N Vijayetha Vardhan

A: The behaviour of the constable in question is deplorable. Kindly complain to the Police Commissioner, Bangalore City. I hope you have noted down the name of the police constable.

Q: I am working in a private firm and I am about to get promoted. Some colleagues of mine, who don't want me to get promotion, have written obnoxious things about me in their blogs. They have made defamatory statements about me. What action can I take?

—K. Nagaraju

A: Section 499 IPC, defines defamation as a publication of any imputation concerning any person, intending to harm that person. The punishment for defamation

is 2 years imprisonment or fine. Since this section is not cognizable, you cannot straightaway lodge a complaint in a police station. You have to approach a Magistrate to take up the case. While lodging the complaint you need not name any body, but can say that you suspect your colleagues. The police will establish the identity of the blogger.

Q: I purchased a mobile phone by placing an order through a web site. When the delivery was made, I made cash payment. After 4 months the mobile stopped working. Despite my complaint, there has been no remedy. Kindly advice.

—V. Shashi Kala

A: If you make purchases through Tele shopping or Internet shopping from reputed companies, you should not encounter such problems. Now you will have to approach a Consumer Court to redress your grievance.

Q: My son is studying in 7th standard in a famous school. He is complaining that one of his male teachers is behaving in a peculiar manner. The teacher is said to fondle him and also touch him at inappropriate places. What can be done?

—Shanta

A: The teacher in question may be having homo sexual tendencies. Please meet the Principal of the School and sort this matter out. What the teacher is doing amounts to an offence. If he does not reform, you may take up the matter with police.

Q: My friend borrowed fifty thousand from me. As security he gave me 2 gold bangles belonging to his wife. He has disappeared and has not paid back my money. I checked with a goldsmith about the bangles he has pledged. They are not gold. Can I file a case of cheating?

—Ramanath

A: Technically the action of your friend amounts to an act of cheating because he has made you part with money by giving an ornament which you believed it to be pure gold. However since he has disappeared, lodging of a complaint against him may not serve any purpose.

Q: I am a senior citizen and live with my wife in an apartment. My children are abroad and I have to visit them for a period of 3 months. Should I lock my home and go or should I engage a private security to look after my house during my absence?

—Mohit Agarwal

A: It is presumed that you are not keeping any valuables in your house and have kept them in a bank locker. It is also presumed that in the event of someone breaking into your house, you have neighbours to notice the same and inform you. If these are taken care of, you may not engage any security guard.

Q: My daughter is studying in 2nd Standard. Last week she came home with a bleeding injury on her head. When enquired, her teachers told me that one of her classmates hit her with a stone which caused the injury. Can we take up a case against the boy?

—Shiamantha

A: As per our criminal laws, no act done by a child is an offence, if the child is below 7 years of age. If the child is between 7 and 12 years of age and if the child has not attended sufficient maturity of understanding to judge the nature and consequence of his conduct, it is also not an offence. Hence you cannot take any criminal action against your daughter's classmate.

Q: I am a NRI and work as a doctor in Canada. Recently I came to India to visit my relatives. During my visit my Canadian passport got damaged. In the meanwhile I got urgent summons to return to my Hospital. When

I went to the airport, I was refused departure stating that unless I produce a proper passport I cannot leave India. Kindly help.

—Tanya Sridhar

A: Since you hold a foreign passport, it is necessary for you to have a correct travel document. Mutilated, torn or disfigured documents are not accepted by immigration authorities. Please approach Canadian High Commission in India and get a duplicate passport issued.

Q: My friend, who is an American, came to Bangalore on a tourist visa which was valid for a period of 180 days. The visa expired 10 days ago and he needs to get back to his country. What should we do?

—Shiva Shankar

A: Let him approach the Foreigners Registration Office, Office of the Police Commissioner, Bangalore City and get his visa extended.

Q: A few days ago two persons came to me and said that they were in financial trouble and that they require money urgently. They asked me to buy a watch in their possession for Rs. 500. The watch in question was Swiss made and I purchased the same. Yesterday some policemen came to my house along with the persons who sold me the watch and asked me whether I have purchased the same. I told them the truth and returned the watch. Now the SHO of the police station is asking me that if I don't pay Rs. 5,000/- I will be booked in a criminal case. What should I do?

—Rame Gowda

A: Receiving and retaining stolen property and knowing that the property is a stolen one is an offence under section 411 IPC. Before purchasing the watch, you should have verified whether it is stolen or otherwise. Since you appear to have purchased the watch without

any ulterior motive, it is difficult to prove a criminal case against you. Please approach senior police officers and complain against the SHO.

Q: I am working with an MNC. Last week I engaged an auto rickshaw to drop me home. The driver demanded extra fare for which I agreed. The driver started going in a longer route for which I objected. He stopped the auto rickshaw on the road, shouted at me, held my hand and tore my salwar. I shouted for help. Many onlookers came and sent me home in another rickshaw. What should I do?

—Jaswant Kaur

A: I hope you have noted down the registration number of the auto rickshaw as well as the license particulars of the driver which is displayed behind the driver's seat. If this has been done, it is very easy to catch the culprit. The action of the auto driver amounts to a criminal offence. Please approach area police station to lodge your complaint.

Q: A large number of four wheelers are getting stolen from our area. Is there a car lifting gang at work?

—C. Venkatesh

A: Many four wheelers which get stolen are used for the purpose of smuggling, joy rides, committing heinous offences etc. Sometimes they are cannibalized and their spare parts sold. If proper preventive steps like installing autocop, steering locks, wheel locks etc are taken such thefts can be prevented to a large extent. Many vehicle owners don't display proper number plates, which is incorrect.

Q: How should the traffic police respond when they see an ambulance with its siren and beacon lights on? Some cops turn off the traffic lights some don't. My friend and I have also witnessed on some occasions ambulances at traffic junctions with siren on (probably

to wade conveniently through traffic) but people in the rear of the vehicle just chatting and laughing.

—Fr. Adolf Washington

A: It is always necessary to give the right of way to an ambulance whether or not any patient is actually present in the ambulance. An empty ambulance might be rushing to a patient's home to carry him to a hospital. For attendants in an ambulance, carrying patients is a chore. Hence you find them chatting and smiling.

Q: Going to another city for some urgent work, I caught an auto at 8.30 p.m to get to the Majestic bus stand. The autowallah asked for one-and-half fare and I agreed as I was in a great hurry. He took me to a dark part of the road near the bus stand. The meter read sixty and so I gave him what I thought was a hundred rupee note. He quickly pocketed it. When I asked for the ten rupees balance, he claimed I had given him only ten rupees. I checked my purse, and found that it was actually a five hundred note instead. We argued but since I was already late for my bus, I had to rush off. If such a thing happens again, would it help if I took him to the police? How can the police decide whether a note found on him is mine?

—Krishna

A: Your case is not an isolated one. Many a time some wicked auto drivers have cheated passengers regarding the fare actually received by them. Whenever you give a high denomination currency note to any person, it is advisable to tell him that you are tendering a 500 rupee note or a 100 rupee note. That way the receiver knows that you are alert. All auto rickshaws have details about the vehicle number, drivers name and other particulars. It is always advisable to note down the same which will help you in lodging a complaint if necessary with the authorities. Now it is too late for you to approach the police.

Q: My neighbour who is from the north works in a software firm. His wife is also a working woman. They have brought a young girl from their native place as domestic help. This girl does not know Kannada. She appears to be less than 10 year old. Can I complain about this to anyone?

—Prathiba. M

A: It is obvious from your letter that your neighbours have engaged child labour. You can alert State Child Rights Commission or Child Welfare Committee. You may just dial 1008 and inform them about the domestic help. They will rescue the girl and keep your name secret.

Q: I received an e-mail making all sorts of imputations against me and my wife, calling me a goonda and calling my wife a female who spoilt her daughter's family. Even though I gave a complaint in the police station one year ago, nothing seems to have happened. Please advice.

—Sathya Narayana

A: The abusive e-mail which you received might have originated from a foreign country and that the police might not have been successful in finding out the IP address of the sender of the e-mail. It seems that this e-mail has been sent by someone known to you living abroad. Since almost one year has elapsed and the culprit has not been traced, the investigation might have been closed.

Q: I am a working woman. I have a small baby. I have appointed an 'ayah' to take care of the baby during my absence. The other day my neighbour informed me that the ayah has taken up a job in our neighbourhood and is taking the baby to her workplace stating my baby as her own. Can I take up a case of cheating?

—Meghamala Sen

A: No criminal case is made out as per the facts stated by you. You can terminate the services of your ayah and put your child in a good crèche. In a recent case an 'ayah' was found begging in a traffic junction with the baby of her employer and in another case, the ayah kidnapped the child. Please be careful with whom you entrust the custody of your child.

Q: I am a working woman I was in love with a person in the past. Later on we separated. Now I am engaged and to be married soon. My ex-boy friend phoned me the other day stating that he is in possession of my nude photographs and if I pay him one lakh rupees he will destroy the photos; otherwise he will send the photographs to my fiancé. What should I do?

—Name withheld on request

A: The action of your ex-boy friend amounts to an offence under Sec 384 IPC and your ex-boy friend can be jailed for a term of 3 years. He can also be punished for an offence under Sec 509 IPC. Please don't agree for any of his demands, but take up a case against him. You may take your fiancé into confidence before taking up action against your ex-boy friend.

Q: When I went to draw some cash in an ATM I found a woman with a young girl present there. The woman asked me to help her draw the money but I refused. She went away. The girl stood near me. As the cash came out of the machine, the young girl grabbed the notes and quickly ran away from the ATM. I tried to chase her but could not catch her. What should I do?

—Purushotham Nair

A: You did the right thing in not helping the woman draw the cash. The ATM card she was having might have been a stolen one and you could have unwittingly been involved in a police case. The woman and the child were acting in tandem. Every ATM will have a camera and certainly the woman and the girl would

have been caught on camera. With this evidence it will be easy for the police to locate the culprits. While operating ATMs please be watchful about your surroundings. Cash vended by the ATMs should be secured immediately and while counting the same be aware of the presence of strangers around you. The doors of many ATMs don't easily open unless you press a button or insert your card. It is not known how the young girl could open the door. You can also alert your bank to secure the door. Please lodge a police complaint.

Q: While I went to my native village last week. I found a number of villagers owning motorbikes. I got surprised and asked one of the new owners about his acquisition. He told me that some days back two persons from Mysore came to the village and sold motorbikes for Rs. 2,000/- and when asked for the documents the sellers replied that documents would be given after the full amount is settled. Isn't this something fishy?

—Sadananda Hegde

A: A large number of two-wheelers are being stolen from various places of the State. The thieves approach innocent villagers and sell the two-wheelers after taking an advance amount and convince the buyer that the additional amount can be paid after the documents are delivered, but they never return. The buyers will have to part with the stolen two-wheelers once the case is detected. Sometimes the thieves sell the two-wheelers to motor vehicle repair shop and the shop keepers in turn sell them to unsuspecting villagers. There is a need for police to create an awareness campaign for villagers.

Q: Can I lodge a complaint through e-mail?

—Satish Chandran

A: At present there is no system of getting complaints lodged through e-mails. Criminal cases are of two kinds; cognizable and non-cognizable. Police are empowered to register and investigate the cases only in respect of cognizable offences. Therefore it is to be examined whether your complaint falls under the cognizable category or otherwise. A large number of cases that come to police station are non-cognizable cases. Therefore to register the cognizable cases that come to police through e-mail some adjustments need to be made. It should however be possible to get this matter sorted out in future.

Q: My daughter aged 7 years is studying in a school and I have engaged an auto rickshaw to take her to school and bring her back home. Two days ago the auto rickshaw driver told me that my daughter was not found in the school. I made enquiries and was told that one "woman" had come to the school saying that she is my daughter's aunt and she took the child away. So far the whereabouts of my child are not known. I have approached the police with no result till now. What should I do?

—Shyamala Shankar

A: Incidents such as these don't happen frequently. There seems to be negligence on the part of school authorities in allowing a stranger to take your daughter away. The school authorities should have telephoned you before letting your daughter go. Since you have approached the police, a missing complaint would have been registered. If your child has been kidnapped for ransom, you will definitely hear from the culprits at which time you can alert the police and get the child rescued. However if your child has been kidnapped for the purpose of begging or other activities the case would be difficult to crack.

Q: I am a permanent resident of Hosur, Krishnagiri

District of Tamil Nadu. I used to travel to Bangalore on my Motorcycle with Tamil Nadu Registration. I had paid Life tax for my Motorcycle in Tamil Nadu. I am facing much trouble from Karnataka Police and RTO guys. They are asking me to pay Karnataka Life Tax (Road Tax) or bribe Rs 500 each time they catch. It's not possible to convince policeman. Is it necessary to pay road tax?

—Jenish George

A: A vehicle registered in one state can ply in another state up to a maximum of one month. If the vehicle is plying in a state for longer period, the vehicle owner is bound to pay Road Tax to the State in which it is used. Normally police officials and RTOs know which outstation vehicle is being regularly used in their jurisdiction. If you use your vehicle sporadically in Karnataka you need not pay Karnataka Road Tax. Regarding demand of bribe, approach Hon'ble Lokayukta, Bangalore.

Q: My father lent 2 lakh rupees on interest to a government employee who is a health officer under BBMP. The employee gave blank cheques for 2 lakh rupees without any date and name mentioned on them but signed by him. Now that the officer has not paid interest from past one year and is refusing to even pay the principal. amount, we have only those cheques given by him. Please advice what's the best way to get our money back.

—Tejes

A: The easiest way to pin down the debtor is to affix your father's name with the current date on the blank cheque given and present the same in the bank. The cheque is definitely bound to bounce. Once it bounces, take up a criminal case. As per the conduct rules, before borrowing money a government servant is expected to obtain permission. You may also complain to the BBMP Commissioner.

Q: Supposing a thief comes to our house and tries to assault us to take away our property, can we attack the thief and repulse him.

—Latha Sudheer

A: Every person has a right of private defence. Also every individual should try to prevent commission of a cognizable offence. While preventing commission of an offence a person can use force on the perpetrator of crime. In a recent case, a criminal entered into a house and tried to kill the father of the house owner. The house owner snatched the weapon of the assailant, attacked the criminal and killed him. It was held that the house owner had used the right of private defence and his action did not amount to murder. Hence to protect your life and property you are empowered by law to use force on a person.

Q: We are reading a lot about cases of snatching of chains and hand bags from women. I am a working woman and I want to know how I can protect myself?

—Sheela Ramani

A: If you have learnt Judo or Karate use them against criminals. If you have not, you can buy a can of pepper spray which is available in the market and which can be kept in your hand bag. You can use this spray on the assailant. Some women carry chilly powder in their bags. You should, however, have the presence of mind to use these against the attacker. Many women meekly submit to the assailant to do nothing.

Q: I work in a BPO firm and mostly work in the nights. I have fallen in love with a colleague of mine. My parents got me married to a person of their choice last year. I don't want to live with my husband. My boy friend has advised me to give a complaint against my husband and in-laws saying that they are harassing me for dowry. Should I give complaint in

the Police Station?

—Name withheld on request

A: If you institute a false criminal case against anybody and misuse the criminal justice system you are liable for prosecution. Please therefore don't heed to the advice of your boyfriend. You can talk things over with your husband and get a divorce through mutual consent.

Q: My neighbour is a government servant. Every day before and after office hours, he gets a number of visitors who come in swanky cars. His visitors appear to be rich persons. I suspect my neighbour is indulging in acts of corruption. Can I approach the local police?

—Name withheld on request

A: Even though the local police can register and investigate cases under Prevention of Corruption Act it is better if you approach Lokayukta in this matter. You may give the details in confidence to Lokayukta officials who will take up a case against the concerned officer if your allegations are true.

Q: When I was at home with my daughter, a person claiming to be a police constable came home and stated that my husband needs to come to the police station in connection with a complaint. The demeanour and talk of the person made me feel that he is not a policeman. Are constables not expected to wear uniform while on duty?

—Parvathi Nair

A: All police officers while on duty are expected to be in uniform. Every constable has an identification number which is worn on his slouch hat. Armed constables [who don't work in police station] also wear a shoulder badge with the alphabets CAR or DAR or KSRP. Civil head constables also wear 3 white stripes on a red background on their right sleeve, where as an armed

head constable wears 3 white stripes on a black background. Only personnel working in Intelligence and CID etc do not wear uniform while on duty. Every policeman is expected to keep an identity card issued to him by the department. You should have asked the policeman who came to your home to show his ID card. You could have also telephoned the concerned police station and enquired whether the policeman really is from that police station. Many a time criminals approach unsuspecting women either wearing police uniform or otherwise and rob them of their belongings. It is therefore necessary that even when a person in police uniform approaches, you should make sure of his identity before doing what he or she asks you to do.

Q: I normally drive during the night. Sometimes police officers stop the drivers to find out whether they have consumed alcohol. What if alcohol is found in the breath of the driver?

—Mukund Srinivas

A: If his blood alcohol exceeds 300 mg /100 ml, a driver is said to be drunk and can be booked. Police usually ask the driver to appear before Court the next day where he can pay a fine of upto Rs. 2,000/- For a subsequent offence the fine may be upto Rs. 3,000/- and the driver is also liable for imprisonment. In Bangalore City alone over 38000 persons have been booked for drunken driving in the year 2009. Since punishment for drunken driving in the existing laws is not severe, this problem is not getting solved. Imprisonment is rarely resorted. If a drunken driver kills a person on the road, he may at best spend 2 years in jail. In the famous Sanjeev Nanda case the accused who killed half a dozen persons was convicted for only 2 years jail term. Unless we have tighter laws against drunken driving, our roads will remain unsafe.

Q: What is Night Beat System? What are the policemen expected to do during their beats?

—Ramanathan

A: Beats mean covering designated area by the policemen. There are 2 kinds of beat. Policeman can remain stationary at one point and observe what happens around them and catch criminals. This is called Lurking Beat. Policemen can be mobile and go across many localities in towns or villages and find out what is happening. Now-a-days in cities we have introduced E-Beat System where in the presence of police officer at any given point is electronically noted so that the authorities know whether the policemen concerned actually covered their beat area or otherwise. Police Department is introducing a new beat system in both urban and rural areas in which citizens will also play an active role. Beat police will be meeting designated members of the public, exchange information and sometimes do beat duties along with members of the public. The intention of beat service is crime prevention, catching criminals and getting criminal intelligence.

Q: I had applied for a passport a month ago. Last week one policeman came to my house along with a copy of my application form and asked many questions. While going back he asked me to give him Rs. 200, which I gladly paid. Is the fee for police verification not covered under the passport fee?

—Ramprakash

A: Whenever a person applies for a passport, the passport office verifies whether the particulars given by the applicant is correct or not. Policemen are expected to ascertain whether the applicant lives in the address mentioned in the application and whether the applicant is facing any criminal charges. Only after the verification, passport is issued. However, some

unscrupulous policemen help persons with a criminal bend of mind to acquire passports by taking bribes. The department has already prosecuted a number of police officers for helping criminals obtain passports, sometimes helping the same person obtain 2 different passports in different names. No police officer is expected to demand money from the passport applicant. You should have complained against the police officer concerned to his higher ups.

Q: I run a small industry and employ people from other states. One of my employees from Bihar approached me last week stating that he does not have a bank account in Bangalore and that he is expecting a huge remittance from his family and whether I could help him by getting the amount credited to my account and give him cash in return. I refused to oblige. Is this not something fishy?

—Panduranga Shenoy

A: You did the right thing. Fraudsters hack into someone's bank account and transfer money to some others' bank account electronically. After the money is transferred, they withdraw the same and vanish. If you had agreed to your employee's request, some big amount would have been transferred to your account. This money would be the result of hacking someone else's account. During the investigation of the case of hacking, police would come to know that you are the beneficiary and would link you to the crime. You would have been unwittingly become a "mole" in this transaction. We have seen some Nigerian nationals approaching persons in India and use their internet enabled bank accounts to credit money secured through hacking the bank accounts of others. They pay 10% commission to the person who facilitates such transfers. Please be wary of such persons.

Q: I run a big restaurant. Last month I noticed that there was a misuse of gas cylinders in my restaurant. Instead of monthly average consumption of 30 cylinders, 40 cylinders had been consumed. I became suspicious and conducted my own enquiry. I found out that my Manager had connived with delivery boys of the gas agency and would return full cylinders from the restaurant showing them as empty after removing the seals. Subsequently, the full cylinder would be sold. Can I lodge a complaint?

—N. Muttu Kumar

A: You can definitely lodge a complaint against your Manager for misappropriating your property. The gas delivery boy would also become liable. However, some evidence needs to be collected. You can keep a discreet watch and catch your Manager while he is doing the Act.

Q: I am an unmarried woman. My elder sister who is 40 years old is a divorcee and has two young daughters. My elder sister's husband has started a blog in which he is writing obscene passages about my sister, myself and my two nieces. I don't want to give a police complaint but want to stop this.

—Name withheld on request

A: The action of your former brother-in-law can land him up to 5 years in jail if he is convicted for this offence. You must approach any police station and lodge a complaint. As per the amended IT Act, Police Inspectors are also empowered to investigate IT Act cases and you need not have to go to Cyber Police Station in Bangalore to register your case. If you don't go to the police station, how can they take action against the culprit?

Q: Recently I appeared for Entrance examination for Post Graduate Medical degree. It was widely talked that

some senior doctors impersonate as the applicants and write the exams. Is this not an offence?

—Dr. Kavitha

A: Your experience reminds me of a scene in the popular movie 'Munna Bhai, MBBS'. Impersonation amounts to an offence under Sec 416 of the Indian Penal Code. Also Karnataka Education Act 1983 prohibits impersonating at examinations. An impersonator is liable for imprisonment up to one year and fine up to Rs. 5,000/-

Q: I am divorcee. My wife has custody of my girl child who is 10 years old. I learnt recently that my wife is involved in a call girl racket. I am worried about my daughter who will be exposed to bad things. Can I make a complaint to the police and get back my daughter?

—Name withheld on request

A: If your ex-wife is doing any illegal act, you may inform to the concerned police who will raid her home and take action against her. If a case is filed against your wife, for keeping a brothel, you may bring this fact to the notice of the concerned court and get back the custody of your daughter.

Q: I regularly see traffic police flag two-wheelers and check documents from the drivers. This is causing lot of inconvenience. Can something be done?

—Vishwanath Badya

A: You will be surprised to know that more than 10% of two-wheeler riders' don't possess driving licenses. Many two-wheeler riders don't have proper documents of the vehicle and many are not even have Insurance Certificates. It is necessary to check such persons to prevent accidents on our roads. You would have observed that a document checking is not resorted during peak hours of traffic. Hence, you should not consider it to cause inconvenience.

Q: The menace of street hawkers and vegetable vendors encroaching footpaths on main roads is growing. It is virtually impossible to walk on footpaths. The local police are either helpless, or are hand in glove with those hawkers. Cannot we do something about it?

—Ramesh

A: I agree with you that footpaths are meant for pedestrians and not for hawking. Under various local laws, footpath encroachers can be prosecuted. Police regularly clear the footpaths of hawkers and book cases but the problem resurfaces since the fines for such offences are low. Unless civic authorities provide separate place for hawkers (incidentally hawkers have a right to their livelihood) this problem will not be solved.

Q: Most of the police stations do not accept complaints stating that the incident has not happened in their area. This causes many problems to the complainants. Can you not find a solution?

—Subhash Yadawad

A: If any complainant goes to a police station with a report of a cognizable crime, the police station is bound to register a case and give a copy of the FIR to the complainant. If the incident has happened in the jurisdiction of other police station, the police station which receives the complaint is expected to transfer the case after registration. If any police station refuses to register a cognizable case, the complainant should approach the SP of the District or DCP of the division who will arrange to get the case registered. The complainant can also approach the courts and get the case registered. Despite the above mentioned legal provisions, many police stations are reluctant to register cognizable cases. Superior officers therefore are devising means to get cases registered at a centralized place. Many district police officers have evolved this

facility. In Hubli-Dharwad, a police vehicle visits various localities regularly, collects complaints from the citizens and gets the cases registered, if the complaints are of cognizable nature. In Amritsar, the complainants can lodge their complaints in boxes that are conveniently placed at important places. In Jalpaiguri of West Bengal, police officers have been motivated to freely register all cognizable cases. Some officers are also devising a method to get the complaints registered through the internet. There is awareness among senior police officers that non registration of crime is serious and they are trying to solve this problem sincerely.

Q: My house is located in a central area of the city. A house adjacent to mine was demolished and a commercial complex came up. Even though ours is a residential area, a gym, restaurant and gift shop are functioning from this building. Visitors of this establishment park their vehicles in front of my gate. It is virtually impossible for me to enter or leave my house in my vehicle. What can be done in this matter?

—Parimala

A: The problem of commercial establishments coming up in residential areas has become serious in major cities. I recall the case of Delhi where courts had to intervene and tackle persons who had converted residential areas into business areas. You can request the local police authorities to declare the road in front of your house as a no parking area. You can request the owners of the commercial establishment to demarcate a separate parking area for their customers. Please approach both the police and civic authorities and if nothing happens you may approach the Court.

Q: I have rented out the first floor of my house to a clinic. The doctor opens his clinic at 5.30 am and closes the same at 10 pm. The doctor has a roaring

practice and his patients come from far and wide. My problem is that the patients and their relatives stand in front of my house, speak loudly, turn on music in their automobile etc. Most annoying thing is many of his visitors urinate in front of my house. What should I do?

—R.B. Chauhan

A: When you rented your building for a business purpose you should have anticipated that you would face such problems. In the first instance request your tenant to vacate the premises or advise his visitors to be considerate to you and your neighbours. If this does not work, you can approach the local police. The facts described by you are petty crimes. You may also approach courts to give you relief.

Q: I had an arranged marriage 1½ years ago and have a son through this marriage. My wife refuses to live with my parents and wants me to set up a separate house. My financial position does not permit this. She has gone away to her parents' house 2 months ago along with the child. She refuses to come back home, refuses to allow me to see my child and has threatened that she will file a dowry harassment case against my parents and myself. Should I get anticipatory bail?

—Puneeth N.

A: Even if you have not taken dowry, if your wife goes to a police station and lodges harassment to her by you and your parents, a case is bound to be registered against you. Merely because a case is registered you and your parents would not be arrested straight away. The investigating officer has to weigh the evidence and then take a decision about the arrest. Therefore, there is no need to rush to courts for anticipatory bail right now.

Q: I was traveling in a day train from Bangalore to Hubli. Somewhere near Tumkur my co-passenger gave my

wife and me "prasadam" from a temple. After we consumed it, we felt dizzy and we must have gone to sleep. When we woke up near Davanagere, we found that our suit case as well as our co-passenger gone. Whether I can lodge a complaint?

—Sridhar Joshi

A: Instances of criminals in the guise of passengers looting away the belongings of train and bus passengers are becoming frequent. It is therefore necessary not to accept food stuffs from unknown co-passengers. Normally food is served as prasadam in order to make it acceptable. Polite refusal is the best prevention. Suitcases and bags need to be chained to the seats or the overhead racks while travelling. It is better not to carry expensive items while travelling. Now that you have become a victim, you may lodge a complaint either in Davanagere Railway Police Station or Tumkur Railway Police Station whichever is convenient. Offences on the railways are investigated by the Government Railway Police and not by other police stations situated in various towns or villages.

Q: I am a married working woman. Ours was a love marriage. My husband is from the north whereas I am from the South. We had a nice marriage till our son was born. After this the personality of my husband changed. He would not allow me to feed my baby nor allow me to be near the baby. We somehow managed and when the baby was 6 years old I decided to live separately. Someone advised us to go for counselling. My husband refused to come for counselling but he was persuaded to attend. During the counselling it transpired that my husband was subjected to sexual abuse when he was a child. After knowing this, I decided to divorce my husband but he is not willing. The case is going on. I am supposed to keep my child with my husband on holidays. I suspect that my

husband is abusing the child. Can police help me?

—Name withheld

A: Sexual abuse of children is a serious offence, even if the child is your own. A case can be taken up against your husband provided there is some element of proof. Have you noticed any behavioural change in your child? Has the child confided in you? This is a very delicate problem. You may approach the court and bring these facts to the courts notice so that your divorce takes place early. If necessary lodge a police complaint against your husband.

Q: The other day I went to my club and had two drinks. When I was driving home, traffic police flagged me and tested my breath. I was tested positive. The PSI asked me to pay a bribe of Rs. 3,000/- stating that if he books a case I will be imprisoned. I paid Rs. 3,000/- for which he gave a receipt for only Rs. 1,000/- and let me go. Is this not corruption?

—Name withheld on request

A: A person who has consumed alcohol is not expected to drive. If he is found drunk, the traffic police are expected to take away his license and other documents and ask him to appear before the court the next day. If he is driving alone, police will ask him to park his car and go home in an auto or taxi. If he has somebody with him who is not drunk and who can drive, police will ask the friend to drive the vehicle. No spot fine is taken from drunken drivers. Since you have a receipt from traffic police, find out the designation of the officer who fined you. Complain against him to the Additional Commissioner of Police, Traffic, Bangalore City.

Q: I had parked my car on the road in front of my house. I noticed that someone had smashed the head lights and tail lights of my car in the night. Can I lodge a complaint?

—Sunil N. Murthy

A: The act of vandalism amounts to an offence of mischief under the Indian Penal Code for which the accused can be imprisoned for a term of upto 2 years. This offence is a non-cognizable one and you may have to approach the court to get the case registered. The chance of detection is very poor.

Q: Last week, after withdrawing two lakh rupees from my bank, I was driving to my workplace. At a traffic signal, two persons riding a motorcycle stood next to me and informed me that oil is leaking from my car and rode away. After crossing the signal, I parked my car on the roadside, got down and bent to check the oil leakage. There was no leakage. When I re-entered my car, I realized that my brief case containing cash had vanished. Where can I lodge the complaint?

—Premanath

A: You have fallen on prey to a very old con trick. The two-wheeler occupants have watched you withdrawing heavy cash, have followed you and made you stop the car and while you had bent to check the leakage, have snatched your brief case. Some other tricksters approach people carrying cash from the bank saying that dirt is attached to their clothes, divert their attention and snatch the cash. Others sprinkle low denomination notes on the ground and when the victim bends down to pick them up, snatch away the bag carried by the victim. It is very necessary to be wary of such tricksters. You can lodge a complaint anywhere. Since you have lost currency notes, it is most likely that the culprits would have spent the amount and you are unlikely to get back the lost money.

Q: When I travel from my home to office and vice versa, I notice a number of traffic violations like signal jumping, riding two-wheelers on footpaths, drivers

speaking on cell phone etc. Can I complain against such people and if so to whom?

—Satish Chandra

A: You can give complaints/suggestions about Bangalore traffic matters through the web site of traffic police at www.bangaloretrafficpolice.gov.in

Q: I am working as a doctor and I have to attend to emergency calls. The other day, I was flagged by a traffic policeman saying that I was speaking on the cell phone while driving. I was using a hands free Bluetooth device and was also concentrating on my driving. As a doctor I have to attend to medical emergencies and have to take calls on cell phone. Despite telling this fact, the traffic police have issued a notice. Is it not unjust?

—Dr. D'Souza

A: As per the MV Act and rules, no one including a doctor can use a cell phone while driving. If there was an emergency, you could have stopped your car and taken the call. Alternatively, you could employ a driver and take as many calls as you want while riding as a passenger in your car.

Q: I am a freelance TV host and appear on Kannada TV channels very frequently. Of late I am receiving SMS from various numbers containing only one message - "I Love You". This has become very irritating. Even after changing my cell phone numbers the messages have not stopped. What should I do?

—Nirmala (name changed)

A: As per the amended IT act, the sender of such message can be booked. Please lodge a complaint in a police station nearest to you. There is no need for you to approach Cyber Police Station since all Inspectors have now been empowered to investigate such cases. It is very easy to trace the culprit.

Q: My mother is an invalid and we have engaged a nurse through an agency to take care of her. The nurse informed me recently that she is two months pregnant and my driver is responsible for it. She is asking us to pay Rs. 50,000/- for an abortion failing which she would file a case against us. We are confused. Please advise.

—Vinodha

A: If the nurse in question developed illicit intimacy with your driver, you are not responsible for her action and are not liable. If she alleges forced sexual intercourse, your driver can be booked for an offence of rape. If theirs was consentual sex, even the driver would not be liable. It is presumed that your nurse is an adult and your driver didn't have sex with her promising her marriage. You need not pay any money to her.

Q: I am married for more than 25 years and have two children. Ever since the marriage, my husband did not permit me to do what I wanted to do. He is very demanding, dominating and suspicious. He does not allow me to go alone anywhere. I look after my family business. Recently, I met a gentleman in my shop and explained my predicament. He suggested me to run away from home and seek divorce. Taking his advice, I took my belongings and some cash, ran away from home and am now living in a PG accommodation. I have learnt that my husband has filed a kidnapping case against the person who advised me to run away. I don't want any harm to come to that gentleman. What should I do?

—Vimala Bai (name changed)

A: Even if a complaint is lodged by your husband, since you are an adult, and you are within your senses, and since you have left home on your own accord, no case of abduction can be established against your friend.

You can state the facts to the police if they approach you..

Q: My husband is a drunkard. He beat me often and life has become unbearable. The last such beating resulted in breaking of my tooth. I don't want to live with my husband anymore. Can I give a police complaint?

—V. Padma (name changed)

A: Causing loss of tooth by beating amounts to causing grievous hurt, which is punishable under the Indian Penal Code. This is also a cognizable offence where a case can be registered and the accused can be arrested. If you give a complaint against your husband, a case will be taken up against him.

Q: I was travelling from Mysore to Mandya in my car. At Maddur, I parked my car and went to a road side hotel to take refreshments. My driver was waiting outside. As I came out of the hotel I noticed one motor cycle rider skidding and falling on the road. I asked my driver to help him. I summoned a police constable who was on duty and put the injured in my car and took him to the hospital. Later on I drove to Bangalore. After a month I received a notice from Mandya Police stating that my car is involved in an accident. I did not bother. A few days later, a policeman came to my residence and wanted to arrest my driver. When I asked the reason, he told me that my driver has dashed against a motor cyclist and caused him injuries. Since I had noted down the number of the traffic police constable whose help I had sought to shift the injured, I explained the facts. Subsequently, Mandya Police closed the case. Now my driver has received a notice saying that the complainant has refuted B-report filed by the police and my driver should appear before the court. What should I do?

—Dr. Devamma

A: We have recently noticed a trend wherein false accident cases are registered against owners of cars and other four wheelers, only with a view to claim insurance. A gang of persons supported by lawyers, policemen and doctors are indulging in getting such cases registered and on the basis of false injury certificates, are getting insurance claims. Most car owners, to avoid further headaches go to court, say that they admit their guilt, pay a fine and forget the incident. Very few people like you fight such false accusations. Since your driver has received summons from the court he must obey the court order. He can explain to the court as to what actually transpired.

Q: I had taken a house on rent and made an agreement with the owner for a period of 11 months. As per the terms of agreement, if I stayed for more than 11 months, I was bound to get the house repaired and painted. I also had paid 10 months advance rent as a security deposit. I vacated the house after staying there for 18 months. The agreement had not been renewed after 11 months. At the time of vacating, my landlord has deducted Rs. 70,000/- stating that it is the amount due for getting the house painted. Can I give a complaint against my landlord for cheating?

—Nanditha R.

A: The facts described by you do not come under the purview of criminal law. You will have to approach a Civil Court for redressal of your grievance.

Q: My son developed a love affair with his classmate and eloped with her to Tirupathi. Both of them are 17 years of age. The parents of the girl have filed a case against my son. Since he is a minor, can he be arrested for any crime?

—Name withheld on request

A: If a person entices a female below 18 years of age

from her lawful guardians, he can be booked for a case of kidnapping for which the punishment is upto 7-year jail term. If your son has had sex with the girl promising marriage to her, an offence of rape is also made out. Since your son is above 12 years of age, he cannot be treated as a juvenile. He cannot also take recourse to the legal provision that he is of immature mind. He may have to face arrest and prosecution.

Q: My parents are aged above 80 years and are living with my elder brother. My brother does not allow them to meet either me or my sisters. My parents are being harassed by my brother by being fed only once a day; not being allowed to use the toilet during day time as it is locked from 9am to 6pm; they are not allowed to make telephone calls; their room is locked from outside; they are not given vital medicines on time. I learnt about this through a letter written by my father which was smuggled out by a visitor to the house. Can I lodge a police complaint?

—Devendran

A: Any person can lodge a complaint of a cognizable case and it need not necessarily be the victim. Unfortunately cases of this nature are becoming more frequent. Elders are frequently subjected to such crimes by their own kith and kin. You may approach elders help line. You may also approach a NGO or you can directly give a complaint to the jurisdictional police station. Your brother and his family members can be booked for wrongful confinement and wrongful restraint.

Q: My 75-year-old mother was going to the temple. On the way, three people accosted her. One of them was wearing police uniform. They told her that some rioting is taking place nearby and it is not safe to wear gold ornaments. They asked her to remove her bangles, rings and necklace and give it to them. When she

gave the ornaments, they put them in a newspaper, gave it back to her and asked her to be careful. When she returned home she opened the packet and found brick pieces and stones in the packet. What should I do?

—Arun N. Shinde

A: Your mother has fallen a prey to an age old trick. A large number of old women especially living in big towns and cities are being tricked by a gang which has originated in Maharashtra. The gang members are fair, tall and handsome. They operate in groups of three or four. Some of them wear police uniform but will not wear a cap. A case of cheating can be taken up against them. Please file a police complaint.

Q: I opened an IT firm in partnership with some friends. One of my employees committed theft of external hard disk (which contains company confidential data) when he was terminated a month ago. He is using the data contained in the disk to contact my clients and spread false news about our firm. He is sending them e-mails making false allegations against me and my company. My firm has lost business because of this. What should I do?

—M. Stephen

A: You can lodge a case against your ex-employee for an offence of theft as well as an offence under Sec 66A of the IT Act 2000. You can lodge a complaint in any Police Station.

Q: I developed friendship with a classmate of mine and we were moving together for about a year. My friend proposed marriage to me but I refused. A few days back, he sent me a CD by post which contained obscene pictures in which my face was put on the nude body of another girl. My classmate wrote that if I don't marry him, he will put the CDs on internet. I am

aghast. What should I do?

—Name withheld on request

A: Since your classmate has created a CD in which your morphed image is put, an offence under IT Act is made out. Also an offence under Section 509 IPC is attracted. Please immediately lodge a police complaint enclosing your classmate's letter and the CD.

Q: I am having a live-in relationship with a friend since the last six months. My friend, who is normally good natured, becomes unbearable when he consumes drinks. Ten days ago when I objected while he was excessively consuming drinks, he took the bottle of whisky and hit me on my head. I sustained bleeding injuries. I went to the hospital and stated that the injury was caused by my accidental fall. Now I want to give a police complaint. Can I do this now?

—Name withheld on request

A: When you went to the hospital to get treatment for your injuries, you should have clearly mentioned the cause of the injury. Since you have mentioned the injuries to be accidental, if you change your version now, the benefit of doubt will go to your boy friend. If you had told the truth at the hospital, a case under Sec 324 of IPC could have been registered. Now it is too late. You could think of invoking the provisions of Domestic Violence Act against your friend.

Q: I had gone out along with my wife for a party held at a farm house of my friend in the outskirts of the city. Both my wife and I had consumed alcohol and I was driving. When we were driving back late at night one Indica car overtook us and blocked the way. The occupants of the car came to us, showed a revolver and asked us to give away our belongings. They took away my wife's gold jewels, our credit cards as well as our cell phones. I wanted to go to the nearest station and give a complaint but my wife said that since I

was driving under the influence of alcohol, police would book a case against me. Hence I did not go to police. However, I informed our bank as well as mobile service providers to stop misuse of the cell phone as well as credit cards. This incident happened one week ago. Can I now give a complaint?

—Rahul Khanna, (Name changed)

A: You are a victim of a case of robbery. You should have immediately reported the matter to the concerned police. Merely because you had consumed alcohol and were driving a vehicle, it does not mean that you cannot be a victim of crime. Even though there is a delay in reporting the incident, at least now you go to police station and lodge the complaint. It is possible to track the culprits if they use the mobile phone stolen from you or your wife. A case of drunken driving would not be booked against you at this point of time.

Q: I was traveling from Mysore to Bangalore in a train. During the journey two burkha clad women were sitting next to me. Since I had gone to Mysore to attend a wedding, I had carried lot of jewels. During the train journey, to be on the safe side, I had put all my jewels in my hand bag and had kept the bag close to me. After I reached home when I opened the bag to keep the jewels in the safe, I found all the jewels missing. What should I do?

—Shantha Lakshmi

A: During your train journey, one of your co-passengers has unzipped your hand bag and has taken away your jewels. It is very easy to open the zipper of a hand bag or a suit case by using a screw driver. You may please go to a Railway Police Station and lodge a complaint. Most women have a habit of keeping their jewels in the hand bag, thinking that the jewels would be safe in the hand bag rather than when worn on their person. This trend is known to many criminals.

Q: A woman in our locality who is running a shop selling Audio/Video CDs, is loading cell phones with obscene X rated Video clips. She is charging Rs. 100 for a clip which runs for about 3 minutes. Can I lodge a complaint against her?

—Subramanya

A: You can certainly lodge a complaint against the woman shopkeeper as her act is punishable under the Amended IT Act. You may tip off the concerned Police Station.

Q: What exactly is meant by registration of a case?

—M. Suguna

A: Registration of a case means taking up investigation of a cognizable offence by the police. Cognizable offence means any offence for which police can arrest without warrant, like murder, kidnapping, theft, extortion, cheating etc. If you go to a police station and give information about the occurrence of a cognizable offence, police is bound to record your information into writing, prepare the First Information Report and commence investigation of the case. As soon as a FIR is drawn up, it can be said that a case has been registered.

Q: I had an arranged marriage six months ago. On the day of the wedding I got a SMS on my mobile phone stating the girl I am marrying is of a loose character and is having a physical relation with someone else. By then I had tied the mangalasutra. My wife is not at all interested in me and we have not consummated our marriage. She is meeting her boy friend regularly when I am not at home. Getting sick of her behaviour, I suggested divorce. She has refused divorce outright and is subjecting me to mental torture. Can I give a police complaint against her and get call details of her cell phone?

—Gangadhar [name changed]

A: If any person has sexual relations with the wife of another man, without the consent or connivance of that man, the person is guilty of an offence of adultery and can be imprisoned for a period which may extend upto 5 years. However, the wife cannot be punished for her act, this is a non-cognizable case and you have to approach the court to lodge the complaint. If your wife is threatening you with injury to your reputation or property, you can file a case under Section 506 IPC. However this is also non-cognizable and you have to approach the Court. The call details of your wife's cell phone can be obtained by the police if they require it for the purpose of investigation.

Q: I am a retired person and live in an apartment with my wife. Through a friend of ours, we appointed a girl as domestic help. The girl told us that her name is Lakshmi and she is from West Bengal. The other day my grandson who had come home accidentally hit Lakshmi. While in pain she uttered "Allah". We got suspicious and asked her about her origins. She stated that she is a Muslim and belongs to Bangladesh. She does not have any papers. What should I do?

—Ram Manohar

A: Before employing any person as domestic help, a lot of verification is necessary. Without knowing the character and antecedents you should not appoint servants. There are any number of reported cases wherein criminals in the guise of domestic help target aged couples. After gaining confidence of the couple by working diligently for three to four months they kill them and run away with the property. Therefore, before appointing domestic help, it is necessary to get their finger prints, photographs and other particulars and get police verification done. Since you have kept a foreign national in your house, you have to immediately inform the local Police Station about your domestic help. They will register a case against her

under Foreigners Act. Many Bangladeshi girls and women are now operating in Karnataka and some of them are in the oldest profession.

Q: My wife has filed a dowry harassment complaint against me and my family in women police station at Mysore, even though we have not demanded any dowry from her family. She states that she will withdraw the case if I agree to give 50% of my assets to her. Local police are not helping. Please help me.

—Aruldhas D.

A: If a complaint of a cognizable case is lodged in a police station, police is bound to register the case and take up investigation. During the investigation the veracity of the complaint is verified. If a false complaint is lodged, a case can be booked against the person who lodges the false complaint. Your wife is bound to provide evidence to the investigators about your accepting dowry. If you are innocent you need not worry. If you feel like, you may obtain anticipatory bail.

Q: In this column sometime ago one person had given you information about confining his parents by his brother. How could you not ascertain the e-mail ID and address of the questioner and rescue his parents? I really pity the old couple.

—Sundaram

A: I get many questions for this column. Some describe real incidents and some are imaginary. Some people disclose their real identity and some want their identity to be hidden. The intention of the column is to offer advice. Insofar as the question regarding confining aged parents, it is not difficult for the police to locate the couple and rescue them. But before any action is taken, it is necessary to ascertain the veracity of the complaint. Many a time innocents have been put to trouble by false complaints against them. That is why

I suggested the complainant to go to the Police Station.

Q: I live in a huge apartment block. I have observed that a number of security guards and others working there are from North Eastern States. Could they be members of outlawed organizations? Who has to check them? I feel insecure.

—P.B. Bangera

A: It is a fact that there is an influx of people coming from North Eastern States to South India. Many come in search of employment. Employers should get a background check of their employees done to rule out that they are not victims of human trafficking or are people wanted by the police. People who run security agencies fall under the Private Security Agencies Regulation Act. One of the Rules framed as per this act is that the Security Agency appointing a guard has to get the character and antedents of the guard verified before employing him. I assume that the Agency supplying guards to your apartment block has got the verification done.

Q: My wife was travelling by air from Bangalore to Mumbai to attend a wedding and was carrying lot of jewellery. She thought that the jewels would be safe if they were put in the checked-in baggage. When she landed at Mumbai airport, her baggage never came to the carousel and on enquiries with the airline staff she was told that it was missing and would be sent to her address in Mumbai. The next day, the baggage was delivered. When she opened it, she found all the jewels missing. We made a complaint to the airlines, but they were least bothered. Can we lodge a police complaint?

—Radhe Shyam

A: All checked in baggage before being loaded into the aircraft are screened and jewellery can be easily

detected through x-ray. Certain unscrupulous persons mark the suitcase and tip off the loaders who steal the valuables. Since your wife did not mention to the airline staff at the time of check in that the suitcase contained valuables, the airlines might say that they are not responsible and cannot reimburse the loss caused. You may take up a case against the airlines in a consumer forum. You must lodge a complaint of theft either at Bangalore or at Mumbai. It is not very difficult to detect this case.

Q: When I recently went to a police station to complain about my neighbour, the SHO listened to me patiently. Meanwhile, my neighbour came and started complaining against me which was mostly half-truths. Upset by the lies, I interrupted. Angered by this the SHO started abusing me and went on to warn me that if I do it again he will use foul language against me and also lock me up. Can an officer threaten me like this?

—Ashwin Naimpally

A: There was no need for you to interrupt your neighbour when he was talking to the SHO. You could have listened to him patiently and rebutted his arguments later. It is necessary for the police to know both sides to the story and you were not facilitating it. The SHO should not have abused you.

Q: My son had gone to Udaipur where he lost his video camera. He wanted to lodge a complaint at Jaipur where it came to his notice. The police at Jaipur wanted him to go back to Udaipur and lodge a complaint. With great difficulty and spending a full day, a complaint was lodged in Jaipur. Now the police in Udaipur have spoken to him over mobile and asked him to go over to Udaipur. They say that they have not traced the camera, and it appears as though it is just a formality that my son has been called. The question is whether my son has to go all the way to

Udaipur, just to fulfill a formality. If he does not go, will the police stop the investigation? Will it be acceptable if he mentions the above difficulties by means of a letter to Udaipur police? What else can be done by my son?

—K.S. Srinivasa Iyengar

A: If the camera is traced by the police, your son has to go to Udaipur to identify it. If not, there is no need to go. Investigation is not stopped if he doesn't go. If the police closes the case as undetected, a notice is issued to the complainant.

Q: I own a Skoda car. Some culprits stole the car's logo last month. I got new one fixed. Last week, it was also stolen. I went to the Police Station to lodge a complaint of theft, but police refused to register the case. What should I do?

—Preeti Agarwal

A: The property stolen in this case is a metallic logo. In its form and looks it is similar to many such logos. It is like someone stealing a bag of potatoes. It is virtually impossible to detect such cases, and even if detected, impossible to prove that the recovered logo was stolen from the complainant and none else. In such cases, and in cases wherein the value of the property lost is meagre, as provided for under Sec 157 of the Criminal Procedure Code, police do not register a case and take up investigation. It is better not to approach the police.

Q: I am an Engineering student. I was in love with a classmate of mine and we had physical intimacy. He has shot some intimate moments we had in his cell phone camera and has shown this to me. Our relationship has turned bad and I asked him to return me the video clips. He is demanding one lakh rupees. I don't have that much of money. Can the police help me?

—Name withheld on request

A: Many young girls have become victims like you because of carelessness. Don't you remember the Delhi Public School MMS scandal or Hassan incident called Mysore Mallige? The action of your ex-boyfriend amounts to an offence of extortion which is punishable under section 384 IPC for which the punishment is jail term for 3 years. You may lodge a police complaint. Please ensure that the video clip does not get circulated to others or put on the internet. If your ex-boyfriend circulates the clips on the net, he will also be liable under the IT Act.

Q: When we go to the police station for some problems, the concerned officers have to help us without expecting anything from us. The other day, one foreigner went to the police station to get the resident proof certificate to renew his visa. The police constable asked his Indian friend to get a ream of paper for writing purpose in the office. The same thing happened when we went to the police station to declare the unexpected death that took place in our campus. After everything was over, the police constable asked our driver to go and get some reams of paper for writing. Does not the government provide the police stations with the necessary writing materials? What is your opinion about this?

—Lawrence

A: All Police Stations have enough funds to purchase stationery. They also have been provided sufficient fund which is to be spent for the purpose of investigation. You should have refused the demand outright.

Q: One of my friends was caught jumping the traffic signal. The Traffic Inspector caught him and gave him two alternatives - either go to the Court and pay Rs. 1,200/- fine or pay a fine of Rs. 600/- on the spot. My friend had only Rs. 200 and told him that he does not

have enough money. The Inspector took the money, pocketed it and allowed him to go free. Can you not take any action on the traffic policeman?

—Pinniti Kalidas Reddy

A: Traffic Police Officers who are authorized to levy spot fine have been provided with Black Berry and it is very difficult to play mischief. Traffic violators who do not have enough money to pay spot fine should opt to go to the Court and pay the fine. In some cities spot fines are collected by the traffic police by swiping the credit card of the offender. This system may also come to Bangalore soon. My advice is not to pay bribe to the traffic police but to attend the Court and pay the fine levied.

Q: I am an entrepreneur. My office phone gets a call from a North Indian incessantly every day. The caller speaks in a language which we don't understand. He does not understand English. Despite repeated efforts to tell him that it is a wrong number, the caller disturbs us at odd hours. Can I give a police complaint?

—Shaji

A: This is not a police case. Why don't you locate a person who can speak the language of the caller and tell the caller that he is dialing a wrong number?

Q: I reside in a purely residential colony. One of our neighbours is a truck owner. Every night his three trucks are parked on the road opposite his house. Because of this, it has become impossible for us to negotiate the road. A school bus which has to enter our road repeatedly honks and only after 4 to 5 minutes, the trucks are removed making way to the bus. We are put to great inconvenience. Please help.

—Ramdas

A: Why don't all the affected residents of your colony approach the truck owner and instil some sense in

him? If he fails to oblige, you may lodge a complaint with the concerned traffic police station.

Q: I was travelling in a night train from Bangalore to Chennai in a sleeper coach. Somewhere near Bangarpet the train stopped for more than 10 minutes. One person who was moving on the track put his hand inside the window and snatched away my gold chain. I found that other members of his gang had snatched ornaments from other sleeping passengers. We raised a hue and cry. We were told that a gang of thieves had stopped the train and had committed robbery. What should I do?

—Rajan Venu Gopal

A: Since the offence has taken place while you were travelling by train, the competent authority to register and investigate your case is the Railway Police. I hope you have lodged a complaint at Bangarpet Railway Police Station. You could also lodge a complaint with Chennai Railway Police. While travelling in the night women should be careful about their jewellery. The percentage of detection of such cases is quite low.

Q: During my visit to a District headquarters recently, my suitcase was stolen. Since I had urgent work at Bangalore, I telephoned the police station stating about the theft. They asked me to come to the police station, but I could not as I had left the place. I came away to Bangalore. I have now received a call from the police station that I should go over there for recording my statement. My question is can't the police use modern tools like the video conference, e-mail etc? Why should we always go to the police station?

—K. Srinivasa Gopal

A: An FIR can be registered by a mere telephonic call. If a Station House Officer receives telephonic information about commission of a cognizable offence, he can reduce the gist of the call into writing and commence

investigation. In your case the same appears to have been done. Probably the suitcase belonging to you must have been recovered and hence you must have been called to identify the lost property, or else the person who committed the theft must have been nabbed and you might have been called to identify him. Though technology has advanced, suitable modifications have not been made in the Criminal Procedures Code. Probably laws would catch up with technology soon.

Q: I entered into an agreement to buy a house. I paid a sum of Rupees thirteen lakhs for which I was given a receipt. I paid the second instalments of Rupees ten lakhs and when I was about to get the house registered, I came to know that the house is attached by a bank for default of loan payment. I therefore asked the owner to return the money. He gave us a cheque. The cheque bounced. I filed a civil suit for recovery of my amount. Can I take possession of the house with police help?

—Nagkumar

A: Before buying any property it is always necessary to find out the title of the same. You have paid an advance without proper verification. Yours is a civil case and police cannot help. You have done the right thing in approaching the Court for recovery of your money. You should have filed a criminal case when the cheques given by the seller bounced. Now you have to await the outcome of the Court case.

Q: I was living in a rented house. Due to financial difficulty I was unable to pay my rents on time. A few days back, my landlord with the help of some local rowdies forcibly entered my house and threw away all my belongings and locked the house. Can I take any action against the land lord?

—Ningappa

A: The act of your landlord in trespassing into your house

and throwing away your property will amount to several criminal offences. Please approach the concerned police station and lodge a complaint against your landlord and others.

Q: One year ago I was beaten up by some rowdies under the directions given by one of my rivals. The rowdies hit me with sticks and with the great difficulty, I lodged a complaint and an FIR was registered. Police officers appear to be friendly with accused and they must have taken bribes. They have closed the case as mistake of fact. What remedy do I have?

—Bhaskar Nambiar

A: After completion of investigation of any criminal case, the Investigating Officer files a report before the concerned Magistrate. If he is able to find any truth in the complaint he will arrest the accused and file a chargesheet. If he is unable to detect the case he will file a report stating that he could not detect the case. If there is no sufficient evidence available, or the case has been filed under some misconception the IO would say that the case has been filed either due to mistake of fact or a mistake of law. Before filing the final report the IO is expected to give a notice to the complainant. After receiving the notice, the complainant can contest in the Court of Law against the claim of the Investigating Officer. If the Court agrees with the complainant it will not accept the report but ask the Investigating Officer to continue investigation. If you have received a police notice, please appear before the Magistrate and refute the claim of the I.O.

Q: I am an unmarried woman. My parents are very anxious about my marriage and are taking me to various Sadhus and temples and are getting poojas and rituals performed. A few months ago they took me to a Sadhu. He made me wear wet clothes and perform homa, wherein only he and I were present.

He tried to feel me and kiss me. I ran away from the place shouting. I told my mother about this incident, but she asked me to keep quiet. I don't want to allow the Sadhu to go scot free. What should I do?

—Name withheld on request

A: Though there are no witnesses to the alleged act, if you lodge a complaint your version would be believed and a case of molestation would be taken up against the Sadhu. You may have to depose in a Court of Law and the Court proceedings can be held in camera. It is better if you lodge a complaint so that the Sadhu would be brought to book and other innocent girls would be saved.

Q: I am working in a BPO. Majority of our colleagues are females. When I went to the toilet the other day I got suspicious that my movement is being watched. When I thoroughly examined the toilet I saw a metallic room freshener holder. When I opened it I saw a tiny camera inside. I came out and informed this to my colleagues and Manager. My Manager tells me that he will throw away the camera and I should keep quiet. Should I not complain to the police?

—Rekha (Name changed)

A: As per the Amended IT Act, if any person intentionally captures or transmits the image of a private area of any person without his or her consent violates the privacy of the person shall be punishable with imprisonment which may extend up to 3 years. Hence you may lodge a case against the management of your Company. Under the IT Act even attempt to fix a camera is punishable under Sec 84.

Q: How much alcohol one can drink and drive. What does it mean to be above the legal limit for drinking and driving? Now-a-days police are booking cases even when we are under the limit, fit and steady to drive.

—Shashibhushana

A: If the blood alcohol level of a driver is above 30 ml for 100 mg of blood, then the driver is said to be drunken and police can book a case against him. The presence of alcohol is detected through alcometer being carried by traffic police. Any person can verify the readings in this meter. I don't agree that police are booking cases on drivers whose blood alcohol levels are under permissible limits.

Q: How should we tackle the issue of daily use of loud speakers by a few religious places in residential areas where this causes intense discomfort? For one thing why do police stations apparently issue blanket permission to such institutions to broadcast from 5am till midnight everyday mindless of severe inconvenience to the residents?

—Anandaram

A: Under the Noise Pollution Regulation and Control Rules 2000, action can be taken against the institutions in question. Under the Karnataka Police Act, a police officer can direct the concerned to reduce the nuisance caused. If the direction of the police is disobeyed, the concerned can be fined and even imprisoned. Please get in touch with the Commissioner of Police, Bangalore. You may also file a writ petition in the High Court. Please also complain to Karnataka State Pollution Control Board.

Q: The complaint of Sri. Devendran published in *Espresso* of March 22 distressed and shocked me. These unfortunate parents of Devendran needed immediate succour and rescue. Could not the DGP have sent his men immediately to the place where these elders were being held captive? Why neither Devendran nor his sister could not or did not raise hell in front of the house of their elder brother and taken the parents out of his custody instead of using your columns for seeking advice?

—K. Sundaram

A: I get many questions for this column. Some describe real incidents and some are imaginary. Some people disclose their real identity and some want their identity to be hidden. The intention of the column is to offer advice. Insofar as the question of Devendran it was not difficult for the police to locate the couple and rescue them. But before any action is taken, it is necessary to ascertain the veracity of the complaint. Many a time innocents have been put to trouble by false complaints against them. Why the brother of Devendran did not rescue his parents is not known to me.

Q: I am a college student and I am in love with a girl. some time back both of us had bunked the classes and I had taken her for a drive and had parked my car near a lake. Some time later two persons came on a motorcycle and said that they are officers from City Crime Branch. They asked me for my driving licence. After they saw that, they said that they will file a case against us for behaving indecently in public and demanded money. Since we did not have money my girl friend gave the ornaments she was wearing and I gave my wrist watch and gold ring to them. They went away. My girl friend does not want to lodge a complaint because her parents do not know about our love affair. I am in a dilemma. Please help.

—Md. Anwar

A: There is nothing illegal if you and your girl friend were merely sitting in a car and enjoying the scenic beauty. The persons who came on a motorcycle might or might not have been police officers. Many a time criminals claiming to be policeman scare young couples and sometimes even unscrupulous policeman also have done so. I feel that you should lodge a complaint in the jurisdictional police station as soon as possible.

Q: I lost my mobile phone 3 months ago near Cantonment

Railway Station, Bangalore in the morning. Please find my mobile as I am a rural student.

—Pavan Kumar

A: I hope that you have already lodged a complaint about the loss of your mobile phone. Normally police don't register a case because the phone has been lost and not stolen. They would also not make efforts to search for the phone. Please talk to your service provider and see whether they could block the use of your phone by giving its IMEI number.

Q: I sold my Maruti Omni van one year ago, following all sale formalities. The buyer has so far not got transferred the vehicle in his name. I have learnt that he had sold the same to some other person. I am receiving notices from traffic police for several traffic violations of my vehicle. I am paying the penalty since I have lost the delivery note. What should I do?

—Pattabhiramaiah H.S.

A: It is always necessary that immediately after the sale of a motor vehicle is effected, the concerned RTO need to be given Form No. 29. You have not done so and you have also lost the document. You immediately approach the concerned RTO and explain the facts to him.

Q: My aged parents who live in an apartment, are continuously harassed by the apartment secretary since my father questions him on various issues. The apartment secretary has written indecent and abusive note about my father and has posted it in the apartment notice board. Recently the secretary has disconnected water supply to my father's apartment. What can I do to prevent such harassment to my old parents?

—K.A. Padmanabhan

A: The action of the apartment secretary in stopping supply of water to your parent's house amounts to a

criminal offence under Section 430 IPC for which the punishment is imprisonment upto 5 years. He can also be prosecuted under Section 501 (b) IPC for defamatory utterances. Your father may lodge a complaint with the jurisdictional police station.

Q: I am an unmarried graduate and I am employed in a company and earn well. One year back I got registered in a matrimonial site. A person claiming to be a businessman from Hyderabad, having an MBA degree and earning one lakh rupees per month contacted me. He said he is an orphan. We both went out for one or two months. He met my parents and they also liked him. We both agreed to get married and exchanged rings. Later on he said that he is in some serious financial problem and asked me whether I could lend him one lakh rupees, I gave him the money. After one more month he asked for some more money which I gave. Subsequently, he took me to Hyderabad with the pretext of introducing me to his relatives and friends. When we went to Hyderabad he booked a room for us in a hotel, wherein he asked me to have sex with him. When I disagreed, he convinced me that since we are going to marry shortly there is no harm in having sex. I agreed. After some time I returned to Bangalore. One fine day he disappeared and his whereabouts are not known. I have lost my money and my honour. What should I do?

—Name withheld on request.

A: Before agreeing to marry a stranger you should have conducted preliminary background check. It is surprising that you don't even know the name, address or the occupation of the person you were going to marry. You may lodge a complaint against the person for an offence of cheating and rape and also Section 493 IPC.

Q: I planned to build a small house in my site and had

necessary approvals for the plan from the municipal authorities. When I was about to start construction my two neighbours objected to it and asked me to leave a space of 3 feet on all sides and construct the house. This is not as per the approval given by the municipality. Can I take police help?

—Sannappa.

A: You may start construction as per the plan approved by the municipality. If your neighbours obstruct you in your work, you may lodge a complaint against them in the jurisdictional police station.

Q: How could the New York police arrest the perpetrator of attempted bombing at Times Square in such a short time? Why our police cannot be as efficient as them? Why many terrors related cases are still not detected in India?

—Shanthanu Singh.

A: The perpetrator of Times Square crime was detected very soon because a vendor who was at the spot noticed smoke coming from the parked car and alerted the police immediately. Quickly police came to the spot and evacuated people in the vicinity and also took action for defusing the bomb. Cameras that were placed near the incident had picked up images of the suspect. Quick verification was done and the culprit was apprehended. Homeland Security in USA has a large data base and cross references and verification are easily made. We are also trying to have similar technological advances. Even with limited technology, Indian police have been able to detect a large number of terrorist cases.

Q: I got my only son married to a fatherless girl who is from a neighbouring state. Socially and financially the girl's family is a notch below ours. I gave an Audi Car and lot of presents to my daughter-in-law and felt

that she was good with my son. Six months back my son informed that his marriage has not been consummated. My daughter-in-law reportedly talks to two of her boy friends on cell phone upto late hours in the night regularly. She does not do any household work and treats her house as a hotel. Now she has suddenly left my son and gone to her mother's place. Her brother telephoned me to say that she wants to divorce my son and we need to pay them Rupees 2 crores. He also said that if the demand is not met, they will file a dowry harassment case against me and my family members. We have not taken a single paisa as dowry. On the other hand we have given her very costly gifts for which I have receipts and I can prove that we have not sought dowry. Should we get anticipatory bail?

—Chandra Kumar

A: If you have not demanded or accepted dowry and if you have proof of giving gifts to your daughter-in-law, you need not worry even if any criminal case is filed against you. However, as a matter of abundant precaution you may go in for anticipatory bail. Your daughter-in-law's brother can be booked for a case of extortion. You should have done a background check of the girl before getting her married to your only son. Please advise your son to file a divorce petition.

Q: I am a housewife and my husband is very well placed in society. The other day one of my friends asked me as to why I am sending her e-mail's asking her to buy Viagra. I was very embarrassed and surprised. I came to know later that some person has been sending emails to all my friends asking them to buy Viagra. How can I find out about the perpetrator of this crime?

—Name withheld on request

A: Sending offensive mails using your e-mail ID is punishable under Sec 66 (C) of the amended IT Act.

Such a person can also be punished under Sec 66 (A). You may lodge a complaint in the jurisdictional Police Station, and they will find out as to who has sent mails using your ID.

Q: I run a small commercial establishment in a residential neighbourhood. My neighbour is upset with us for this and she always creates a scene whenever customers visit us. She shouts at them and sometimes throws water on their clothes; she also throws garbage in our premises; she has put old shoes, broom sticks in our premises and also she has allowed sewage water from her toilet to run into our front door. Can I lodge a complaint against her?

—Shobha

A: Police can take action against your neighbour for an act of mischief. However her action amounts to a non-cognizable offence and you will have to approach the Court for a case to be registered against her. Action can also be taken against her under the Karnataka Police Act but it will be a petty case. Complain to your jurisdictional police station.

Q: I participated in an auction (conducted by the Debt Recovery Tribunal) of a Coffee Estate and was the successful bidder. The original owner who is in possession of the Coffee Estate is threatening me that if I enter the estate I would be killed. Should I take police help to enter the estate? Will they help me?

—Aravind

A: Since you are the highest bidder in the auction, it is presumed that the Tribunal would hand over the vacant possession of the land along with its clear title to you. You need not worry about the threat of the owner of the Estate who has lost it because of non payment of dues. Since he has threatened to kill you, you may approach the local police and lodge a

complaint of criminal intimidation. If need be you may take their help before you occupy the new property.

Q: I possess a site in Bangalore which was allotted to me by a Housing Co-Operative Society in 1984. I have all the relevant documents pertaining to this site. I am also paying property tax regularly. I could not construct the house due to domestic problems. During 2004, the original land owner, from whom the society bought the land, displayed a notice quoting Supreme Court Judgment, stating that he is the owner of the property and trespassers will be prosecuted. He also threatened me with dire consequences, if I enter the site premises. Can I seek police protection to take possession of my property? There are many who are affected.

—TS Suryanarayana Rao

A: When you bought the site in 1984 and when your fellow allottees constructed houses on their sites, didn't the "original" owner object? Why did he keep quiet for 20 years? Why don't you go through the Supreme Court judgment and know the real facts of the case? Has the owner filed any criminal case against you and others for trespassing? Unless these facts are known, police protection cannot be taken for granted.

Q: Four months ago my aunt gave her house on rent to a family consisting of 3 women. At the time of discussion, they agreed for an advance of 10 months rent and a rent of Rs. 7000 per month. The agreement was to be made at the time of giving advance. This advance was to be given just before they occupied the house. But when they arrived with household items they did not pay any advance nor my aunt made an agreement. Out of sympathy towards the 3 women she rented the house as they promised to pay the advance the next day and make agreement. For over a month they kept on postponing due to one reason

or the other. When my aunt insisted either they pay up advance and rent or vacate the house, they went out never to return. The mobile number they had given is now switched off. How do we get this house vacated and let it out to others? And how do we get these people booked for cheating so that they don't do this to others?

—Saragur Bushi

A: It was foolish on the part of your aunt to allow the tenants to stay in her house without getting advance rent. Since no agreement has been made you cannot claim that they have cheated you. Since the tenants have already vacated the house, there will be no problem for your aunt to lease the house to others.

Q: Although we have strict rules on physical fitness of candidates for selection to police force, by and large, most of them lose their shape within few years after wearing the uniform. Do we have adequate training programmes for officers and men and are we implementing the physical fitness guidelines in letter and spirit? Are we monitoring the physical fitness and readiness among the officers and men on regular basis?

—Sukumaran

A: I have to frankly admit that we are not implementing and monitoring physical fitness standards for our officers and men, once they join the force. Earlier we used to have regular parades and drill etc for our colleagues. Due to heavy work load, parades are not held regularly now-a-days. The Police Department has installed gyms in all district police offices and Commissionerates. However many of our colleagues are not making use of this.

Q: A writer has published an article which is clearly pointing towards my caste. (I belong to Scheduled

caste). I want to file an FIR against the writer and newspaper but police are not co-operating. Please suggest how I can take up a case.

—Santosh Shirgaonkar

A: You may lodge a complaint in any police station. If they refuse to register an FIR, you can approach either the SP of the district or the Commissioner of Police. You may also lodge a complaint with the Superintendent of Police, Directorate of Civil Right Enforcement, Bangalore.

Q: Sir, I would like to know that before making an area or road one way and no parking, is there a provision to notify the general public or is there any notification order issued for it. In case if it is issued, how could the general public know about it?

—Mahesh Bhandari

A: Before declaring a road as fit for one way traffic or before declaring a zone as No Parking Zone, a notification needs to be issued by the Police Commissioner or District Magistrate to seek objections from the public. Affected parties may submit their objections and after considering the same the authority will declare a road as one way or as a No Parking Zone. Notification will have to be published in the Official Gazette and sometimes in newspapers too.

Q: Is it necessary to record the statement of any accused before or after arrest? Can such statement be used against the accused?

— Shilpa R.

A: Normally, the Investigating Officer questions suspect/accused of any case in order to know how that crime committed. Based on this knowledge the Investigating Officer proceeds with investigation of the case. However, a statement of accused before a police officer implicating himself has no evidentiary value in the

Court. But, if the statement of the accused leads to discovery of facts and recovery of any incriminating material, to that extent the statement is admissible. For example, if a person accused of murder, states before the Investigator that he has murdered A with a knife and that he has concealed the knife behind a bush, and the police recover that knife, that part of the statement of the accused which leads to the recovery of the knife is admissible as an evidence.

Hence, recording of the statement of an accused is done to help the Investigating Officer in the investigation of the case and collection of evidence. In certain acts like Prevention of Terrorism Act, confession made before a police officer was admissible. However, this act which was enacted in 2002 was repealed in 2004.

Q: What are the legal defenses available to an accused?

— Ramesh Malhotra

A: When an accused is being arrested, the accused has to be facilitated to contact his advocate. On some occasion during the questioning of an accused in custody, an advocate for the accused can be present. The accused has to be produced before a magistrate within 24 hours of his arrest. The human rights of the accused cannot be violated by the police. An accused cannot be subjected to torture. Only in rare cases an accused is handcuffed. If the offence committed is bailable, the accused needs to be released on bail.

Q: Do police record the statement of an accused on video camera or they simply write down his statement?

— Asha

A: Many a time an Investigating Officer records the statement of the accused on Video/Audio tape. However, such tapes cannot be used during the time of trial.

Notes

Notes